Moral Education

Moral Education

Norman J. Bull
St. Luke's College of Education, Exeter

Beverly Hills, California
SAGE PUBLICATIONS

For information address:

SAGE PUBLICATIONS, INC.
275 South Beverly Drive
Beverly Hills, California 90212

Printed in Great Britain

Standard Book Number 8039-0039-2

Library of Congress Catalog Card Number 77-101419

Contents

Part One
Stages of Development

I
Morality

Stages and Levels

The term 'morality' derives from the Latin plural *mores*, meaning 'manners' or 'morals'. We use it to mean the generally accepted code of conduct in a society, or within a sub-group of society. Thus, we speak of an individual as leading 'a moral life', or of 'public-school morality'. But we also use the term, secondly, to mean the pursuit of the good life – and that is by no means necessarily the same as following the accepted social code. Indeed, moral progress has always been made by individuals who have gone against the accepted morality of their day, and who have generally suffered for doing so.

At once, then, we begin to recognise that there are different levels of moral behaviour. We may illustrate them more fully from driving a car. At the lowest level, a man may drive with complete disregard for anyone else. His sole concern is his own pleasure, limited only by care to avoid doing himself injury. His sanctions or controls are simply pleasure and pain. At a second level a man may drive with care, but only from fear of the law and of the consequences of breaking it. At this level the sanctions are punishment and, its obverse, reward. At a third and higher level a man may also drive with care, but motivated by concern for others and for his reputation among them. Here the sanctions are social praise and social blame. At a fourth, and highest level, a man may drive with care, motivated solely by his own inner principles of conduct. He is dependent neither upon the external constraint of law nor upon the external force of public opinion. His overriding concern is not simply living with others, but living with himself – for his sanctions are internal. They are self-praise and self-blame.

Here, then, are four broad levels of moral conduct. While they may be analysed and defined with far greater subtlety and precision, they serve as a yardstick for the study of moral behaviour. The first may be called pre-moral. The second is essentially an external morality. The third is part external and part internal. The fourth is wholly internal.

While these four levels serve as a general framework, we must be aware throughout of the infinite complexity and variety in moral motivation. Each individual behaves at different times and in different situations on different levels. Indeed, a driver may act upon all four levels on one and the same journey, as the circumstances change. Again, so complex are the roots of moral behaviour that these levels are often intertwined. A driver may be hard put to it, at any given moment, to give one single motivation for his driving with care.

But not only are these the four main *levels* of moral conduct. They are also the broad *stages* through which a child develops into a moral being. We must at once define in what sense we may use this term 'stage'. We are certainly not thinking of a bus progressing along a fixed route from one fare-stage to the next, so that each stage is left behind at a given moment and a new one reached. We are thinking, rather, of the complex human personality. A 'stage', in this context, is a broad period of development, not an exact distance between two fixed points of maturation. Such stages, secondly, may and do overlap within the individual. In particular, they may run parallel in differing contexts and moral situations. Thirdly, they will naturally vary from one individual to another, depending upon the variable factors shaping both the individual and the environment. Above all, as we have already observed, all these stages may survive into adulthood, where we may see them as different levels of moral conduct.

Moral Judgement

It is in terms of these four broad stages that we may seek to understand the development of the child in the moral sense. But how are we to secure evidence? The difficulties are immense – and they form one reason for the comparative neglect of such study in the past. Psychoanalytic theories have the advantage of not being susceptible to scientific investigation. Any other type of study is open to serious criticisms. Thus, it can be charged with being inherently subjective – assuming that there can be such a thing as pure objectivity in any study of man. Even the framework of development that is adopted

may make subjective assumptions. Any results achieved may, therefore, be suspect – and, in so complex and fluid a field as the moral,
solid statistical findings are not easily come by.

One approach would be to observe and to analyse the behaviour of
children in concrete and normal – if fabricated – moral situations. A
massive piece of such empirical research has been made (Hartshorne
& May, 1928-1930), but it has small value today. Another, and far
more dynamic, approach is that pioneered by Piaget (1932). In
painstaking interviews with small groups of children, he sought their
attitudes to the games they played, and their judgements upon stories
of moral situations familiar and relevant to them. Their moral judgements, within different areas, were analysed to produce a stage
sequence of development. A somewhat similar approach was used
in the research from which this book derives.

1 Moral Judgement and Moral Behaviour

Such an approach is open to criticism. First, what relationship is
there, if any, between moral judgement and actual conduct? How far
are the child's judgements, however genuine, sure to be acted upon?
If no association can be proved, what is the value of such judgements?
And, in particular, what is the validity of any developmental pattern
derived from them?

No claim could be made for strong correlation between moral
judgement and moral behaviour. Indeed, statistical substantiation for
such relationship would not be easy to achieve. Even if the individual
knows the right thing to do, so much depends upon motivation, the
actual situation, and – according to some adolescent girls – even
mood.

Yet it remains true that moral knowledge and understanding are
prerequisites of moral action. No one can act upon a moral principle,
or precept, or rule, unless he is first aware of it. He must, for example,
have learnt respect for the property of others if he is to know that he
should resist the temptation to take it when safe opportunity offers.
He must have learnt something of personal relationships, and of
respect for the other person, if he is to know that he should refrain
from telling a lie when it would be to his own advantage to do so. No
one can practise the Golden Rule of reciprocity unless he is aware of
it – and, above all, has understanding of its application to concrete
situations.

꘭ Moral judgements derive from moral concepts. These have matured, with time and experience, and their roots go deep. It can at least be held that they furnish evidence of potential moral action; and the more so as moral principles become interiorised and a sense of guilt becomes a reality of moral experience and so a moral control.

2 *Moral Judgements purely Cognitive?*

Emphasis upon 'knowledge' and 'understanding' raises a further question. Are not moral judgements purely cognitive? May not the child being tested be playing a purely intellectual game – giving theoretical answers to theoretical questions? What possible indications of his true moral concepts can be given by such judgements? May they not be totally unrelated to the powerful emotional and motivational factors that must profoundly affect his actual conduct?

Spurious judgements, bearing no relation to the child's own attitudes, are the more likely if he is asked direct, personal questions, whether he is seeking to please or to conceal. They are also likely if the child, even if presented with a concrete though imaginary situation, is asked what the child involved in it *ought* to do. The development of projective psychology offers tools that bypass such defects. Tests can be devised picturing a moral situation into which the child 'projects' himself. By identifying himself with the child portrayed, putting himself in the child's place, he unwittingly reveals his own inner attitudes. Projection tests, being both indirect and impersonal as well as concealing their purpose, are far more likely to tap genuine attitudes.

Much more important, however, is the *nature* of moral judgement. At least some psychologists hold that all thinking is emotionaliy toned. It is certainly strongly so in the moral field. The responses of children of all ages to moral situations involving what they regard as the greatest evils are far from being coldly cerebral. A boy of 9 years, describing guilt, says,

'Your mind goes all sort of beating fast.'

A boy of 15 years gives a terse definition of conscience:

'Every rotten thing you do sticks in your mind.'

A girl of 17 years holds that

'Lying is all right for reasons of love.'

Moral judgements, it appears, are orectic as well as cognitive. They involve, that is to say, not only the mind, but also appetite and desire, feeling and striving, emotion and will. They involve the person, not simply his mind. When elicited from areas of deep, moral concern, they stem from genuine, often deeply held attitudes, and powerful motivations.

Moral Situations

We have already had to make reference to the actual situation, in terms of both moral behaviour and of moral judgement. The car-driver will judge the changing situations and vary his actions accordingly. The child's judgements can only effectively be elicited in terms of concrete, if imaginary, situations.

Every moral judgement is made within the context of a concrete situation. It will be shaped and moulded – though not determined – by the situation. Just as history never repeats itself, save in broad patterns of similarity, so moral situations are never identically the same, save in their broad patterns of similarity. The implications of this situational factor are far-reaching, and it will be one of our major concerns.

The gravest defect of traditional moral education has been its teaching of blanket moral principles ('Thou shalt not . . .'), with small, if any, reference to concrete situations. Transfer of learning was assumed. But there is both generality and specificity in the moral life. There must, on the one hand, be general principles – of honesty, truthfulness and so on. We assume this in daily life, when we say a certain man is 'honest' or a certain woman 'trustworthy'. Indeed, without it communal life would be impossible. But 'circumstances alter cases'; the general principle must be adapted to the specific situation. The stern moralist, insisting rigidly on the principle, subordinates persons to rules and love to law. It is the application of the principle to the situation, and above all the derivation of the principle from situations, that must be the basis of effective moral education.

The adolescent grapples, often with small help, with shaping the principle to the situation. Would it be right, for example, to lie to the teacher by not telling on a friend?

'No. But I wouldn't betray my friend. I can't say "trust" because you are breaking someone's trust in lying. Friendship is sticking by someone.

Again, is lying always wrong?

'It's all right to lie if you feel you would hurt someone if you did not.
'Hurting people is more serious than telling white lies.'

Here the principle is being adapted to the situation. Law is being
subordinated to love.

Moral judgements are not made in a vacuum. The situational
element is a vital factor in each such judgement. This is not to hold
– as 'situation ethics' appears to do – that judgement is determined
by the situation. Judgement is the application, and therefore adaptation, of principle to situation. The principle must be known, and the
situation assessed. Both are involved.

Judgements will therefore vary from one type of situation to
another. It follows that, in testing, judgements must be sought from
a variety of situations – just as, in moral education, experience must
be given in a similar variety of situations. It follows, too, that, in
seeking to trace development in moral judgement, we must bear in
mind that the individual may be at different stages in different areas
of moral concern.

Variable Factors

Varying stages of moral judgement in the child and varying levels of
judgement in the adult both reflect differences in the shaping of moral
concepts. Their complexity, as well as their variety, suggest the
different influences at work. These vary from one individual to
another; and these variable factors must be taken into account in
seeking to trace development. Key variables are: relationships in the
home; the pattern of discipline in the home; the school environment;
the socio-economic environment; religious influence; intelligence;
and, by no means the least significant, sex. All such factors are
involved. All are threads contributing to an intricate moral pattern.

It follows that no part of the total environment can be ignored. No
part of it can opt out of moral responsibility. Certainly no parent or
teacher, or other adult in relationship with children, can deny moral
influence. Even impersonal contacts play their part. We find, for
example, that the ideals – if not idols – of many adolescents are the
glamorous and successful young adults, known from the film and
television screen, taking the place of ideals from literature and history
of previous adolescent generations.

It follows, too, that we are by no means narrowly concerned simply with ethics. Certainly ethical concepts are involved. But we are no less concerned with the relevance of psychology and sociology, in particular, to the process of development. No one discipline by itself could do justice to so complex a study as that of moral development – if, indeed, to any human concern in our complex modern world.

Research Evidence

The evidence for this developmental account of moral judgement was derived, in the main, from a research project (1964–7). The subjects were 30 boys and 30 girls of every other year of age from 7 to 17 years inclusive – a total sample of 360. Sex differences could therefore be clearly observed throughout. Care was also taken to ensure as random a sample as possible, representative in terms of intelligence and socio-economic background.

1 The Tests

The main body of the research consisted of individual interviews, using visual projection tests. Their themes were the evils known to be of greatest significance to children of all ages – murder, physical cruelty, stealing, cruelty to animals, and lying. The test concerned with cruelty to animals was not analysed. An additional test was included concerned with cheating – a very subordinate and artificial 'crime' to most children.

Four visual tests were analysed. The first, the Value of Life Test, embracing the evils of murder and physical cruelty, showed a child drowning and crying for help to the lone child on the bank. The Cheating Test, concerned primarily with cheating in the classroom, but also with cheating at games, followed. The Stealing Test showed a child alone in the school cloakroom with the opportunity of taking something from an open satchel or bag. The final test, concerned with lying, used the same, highly evocative cloakroom scene, together with a portrait of father or mother, according to the subject's sex, asking questions.

In addition, six written tests, administered to groups, supplied further evidence in other areas. They included the Ideal Person Test, asking both for the identity of the ideal and reasons for choice; a test eliciting the chief vices and virtues, as seen by the subject; a test on attitudes to punishment; a projective Sentence Completion Test, seeking to tap attitudes in various areas; and two tests requiring judgements upon varied moral situations.

2 The Region

The research was undertaken in towns of the South-West region of England. While its towns are by no means insignificant, the South-West remains a predominantly rural and agricultural area. The question immediately arises: how far can a developmental study, made in such an area, be representative of the country as a whole? How far, for example, would it be true of young people in the great conurbations?

Added point is given to this question by evidence found in the statistical survey, *Religion and the Secondary School* (S.C.M. Press, 1968), if we may assume for the present some broad relationship, in a cultural setting, between religious influence and moral outlook. The regional factor was found to be a key influence in shaping attitudes: '. . . the region within which a school is located is probably the most important factor influencing the attitudes of its pupils . . .' (ibid., 68). More particularly, while London is at the foot of the scale of mean 'attitudes' scores, and also of the scale of mean 'religious practice' scores, the South-West is second only to Wales at the top of both scales (68 f.). Thus, in extreme contrast to the London conurbation, . . . 'the Religious Education given in the South-West may well be successfully feeding on, and feeding into, the general cultural religious influences in that region of the country . . .' (70). Moreover, 'It is not merely a question of conurbation versus countryside; among both such groupings actual regional differences make themselves apparent, and (generally speaking) the nearer one gets to London the less favourable the attitudes towards Christianity become' (140).

(*a*) *Church Attendance* In terms of church affiliation, 35% of our sample had no church connection in our youngest age-group of 7 years, the peak age of church attendance. The progressive decline was from 60% regular attendance at 7 years to 18.3% at 17 years, with the peak decline between 13 and 15 years. We found evidence of strong association between church affiliation and positive religious attitudes; but this, of course, may mean no more than that only those do attend church for whom it has real significance. Thus explicit religious influence was by no means universal.

(*b*) *The Ideal Person Test* One regional contrast of relevance and interest can be made. It derives from the Ideal Person Test, used now for seventy years, in which subjects are asked to nominate the person they would most like to be, and to give reasons for their choice. The most striking development over the years in results from this test is the increase in the number of young people who choose to remain themselves. Overall, 20.3% of our sample preferred to remain themselves, the sex difference being small. Of such responses, 65.7% came from the 15 and 17-year age-groups. Thus, 40% of these two mature age groups (boys, 38.3%; girls, 41.7%) chose to remain themselves. These subjects gave positive, healthy and mature reasons for their choice. Nor were they characterised by lower levels of intelligence. Now we are able to compare this finding with results from the use of the same test in a study made of 250 young London workers between the parallel ages of 15 and 18 years (E. M. & M. Eppel, 1966). Here there was a stronger sex difference in subjects choosing to remain themselves (boys, 37%; girls, 52%), although the boys' figure is almost identical with our own. But the combined figure of 44.5% from London contrasts with our figure of 40% from the South-West. This increased figure from London at least rules out any suggestion that subjects from the South-West, choosing to remain themselves, indicate lethargic content with a sleepy rural way of life.

(*c*) *Piaget's Study in Geneva* Piaget's pioneering study of development in moral judgement was made among 'children from the poorer parts of Geneva' (1932, 37). His whole thesis was derived from so limited a sample, and this is one of the notorious criticisms of his work. He himself recognised that 'in different surroundings the age averages would certainly have been different' (op.cit., 37). But such differences of detail were not allowed to affect his main theory of stage development in moral judgement; and this is legitimate if there are stages through which a child must pass on the road to moral maturation, however those stages be defined and explained. Thus Piaget derived a universal theory from a very limited 'regional' survey. His insights into the dynamics of development inspired subsequent studies that have seriously weakened his theorisings. But his work remains the key study of this area.

The point of interest, here, is that Piaget found the key turning-point in development towards maturity in moral judgement at about the chronological age of 11 to 12 years. In our study in the South-

West we found the climacteric stage of development to appear between 11 and 13 years. If we hold such development to be shaped by inner growth, as well as by external influences in the environment, then a pattern of sequential stages becomes a legitimate picture of the process.

So far as potential regional differences in our own country are concerned, substantiation could only come from parallel studies in other areas; and, in particular, from the great conurbations.

A Developmental Study

It will already be evident that our main interest is in tracing development in moral judgement, rather than in seeking to achieve a precise, statistical survey of so complex and fluid an area. Judgements vary from individual to individual, from stage to stage – above all, from one moral situation to another. Indeed, the very concept of 'moral judgement' may be a blanket term covering a number of related factors. But we can at least seek out a broad pattern of development from analysis with children of varied moral situations.

The four stages, or levels, used as the framework of this study were first delineated by McDougall in 1908. His lucid, if somewhat static, picture of development can be valuably amplified by the dynamic insights of Piaget, without accepting his theorising; and by studies inspired by both pioneers.

2
Pre-morality

The Origins of Conscience

If, for the present, we use the term 'conscience' to mean a developed, interior morality, the question at once arises – what is its origin? No study of development in moral concepts is possible unless we assume that the child is born without moral consciousness, without a conscience. This is, in fact, a modern assumption, and hence the lack of studies of such development before about 1900. It had previously been held that the child was born with a conscience. This tradition, allied with a rigid dogma of original sin, meant that the erring child was deliberately delinquent. What we now recognise as his innate immaturity, his egocentricity, was therefore taken as criminal, if not sinful. Hence the enormities of cruelty perpetrated against children in educational history.

To say that the child is born without a conscience is not, of course, to say that he is born without moral potential. But it is to realise that he does not come into the world with a ready-made set of moral concepts, any more than with a mature mind or body. Growth is the law of life, and there must be moral as well as physical and mental growth. There is no evidence for such a built-in 'faculty' as an innate conscience. Nor, indeed, would a static inner code of conduct be of much use in coping with the manifold and variegated moral situations of daily life, growing in complexity with increasing age.

1 Feral Children

Conscience, then, must be a social construct, developing as part of normal growth. If we wished to prove this, we would need to isolate new-born children from all human society and observe their development. Such an experiment would, of course, be unthinkable and intolerable.

But such evidence is available from attested cases of feral children, brought up by wild animals. Whether deliberately 'exposed' at birth or accidentally lost in early childhood, they have known no human society. Deprived of human society, they never become human; they are, in fact, bestialised. Neither in body or mind, least of all in moral consciousness, have they realised their humanity; and when brought into human society they wither away. Here is ample proof that human society shapes human personality, including moral consciousness.

2 The Psychopath

A second proof that conscience is not inborn is the psychopathic personality. This is a type of personality lacking in moral consciousness. Such persons may be placed along a continuum, according to their degree of moral deficiency. The complete psychopath is a 'moral imbecile', totally lacking in any moral sense, totally unaware of any moral obligation. In short, he has no conscience. He acts purely upon impulse.

The causes of such moral deficiency are complex. Environmental factors may play their part. A defect in the nervous system may hinder or prevent normal processes of conditioning. Recent research among extreme cases of criminal psychopaths gives evidence of genetic abnormality; and already such evidence has been brought into criminal proceedings at law.

Whatever the causes of the psychopathic personality, its existence provides further, if sorry, proof that conscience is not innate.

Moral Development

The child, then, is born without a conscience as such. He is neither moral nor immoral, but simply amoral. Any moral sense that he is to achieve must come from his society.

But, of course, most individuals achieve *some* moral code. While the codes vary from one society to another – and indeed within a society, in its sub-groupings or sub-cultures – all are underlaid by a sense of moral obligation. It is this sense that is universal. It is the supreme characteristic of man as such. Indeed, it is the unique definition of humanity. It is also the answer to those who argue that, since moral codes differ, all morality is relative, and therefore the individual may choose to follow any or none. The codes differ: they are relative. The sense of moral obligation undergirds them all : it is absolute.

What, then, is the origin of this sense of moral obligation? To be universal, it must obviously be the result of natural processes – not of something imposed artificially from without. There are four such processes. The child begins by imitating the actions of those closest to him, normally parents. Then, through the subconscious process of suggestion, he absorbs their feelings and mental attitudes. Through the process of identification, he incorporates their personal character-istics; he impersonates them. Finally, the impersonated character-istics become his own, forming his own inner ego-ideal, his picture of himself as he should be.

It is this ego-ideal that is the moral self, the source of the universal sense of moral obligation. But it is in daily conflict with the ego, the natural self, with all its instinctive needs and desires. Hence the unending struggle within the individual that is so characteristic of man, and is, therefore, the basic concern of his religions. Yet it is this moral self that raises man above the animal creation. For it gives him in addition his unique self-consciousness; the self-criticism that we call 'conscience'; and the self-control that we call 'will'.

These four processes are wholly natural. Each, that is, has its own biological purpose. Thus, through both imitation and suggestion the child absorbs much that could only otherwise be learnt by hazardous and lengthy experience. Identification with others has similar value in developing the sympathy for, and the sensitivity to, other persons that lie at the root of social life – and, therefore, of morality.

The child is not born with a built-in moral conscience. But he is born with these natural, biologically purposive capacities that make him potentially a moral being. The nature of his morality will depend upon those around him – upon, that is, the identifications that he makes. For not only the capacity for identification, but also the identifications made in childhood persist into adult life. They shape character.

Now it is about the age of 7 years that the child enters upon the period of development that Piaget terms the 'stage of concrete opera-tions' in his developmental psychology. By 'operations' Piaget means cognitive actions that are no longer random, but are becoming related in an organised system. They now form a definite structure, a net-work of actions that enable the child to classify. In the earlier, 'pre-operational stage', from about 2 to 6 years, the child has no concepts as such, his thinking being intuitive, symbolic, and lacking in ability to understand relationships between cause and effect. But from about seven years the child is able to develop genuine concepts, although his thinking is limited to concrete objects and events in his immediate environment, experienced through his senses. It has no capacity as yet for abstract concepts. We therefore began testing with the 7-year age-group in seeking to trace the development of moral concepts. We continued into and beyond Piaget's 'stage of formal operations', from about 12 to 15 years, when the mind develops the capacity for abstract thinking and generalization. No longer limited to the concrete and the real, the adolescent can think in terms of hypotheses and propositions.

The Pre-moral Stage

Piaget begins his pioneering study of moral judgement with a comprehensive definition: 'All morality consists in a system of rules, and the essence of all morality is to be sought for in the respect which the individual acquires for these rules' (Piaget, op.cit., 1). The Greek *nomos* ('law' or 'rule') is therefore a fitting basis for the terms that we may use to define our four stages. Briefly, they are: anomy (without law); heteronomy (law imposed by others); socionomy (law deriving from society); autonomy (law deriving from the self). Piaget acquired from Kant the terms 'heteronomy and 'autonomy' for his stark contrast between an external and an internal morality.

The child, we have seen, is born in a state of amorality – or, as we may now term it, anomy. But we have also noted the natural capacities that form his moral potential. Since the normal child is going to develop some form of morality, we may speak of this first stage as that of pre-morality.

This is essentially the stage of purely instinctive behaviour, with pain and pleasure as its only sanctions or controls. There is some learning involved here, if only in adapting behaviour according to experience of pain and pleasure. But it is, broadly, that of the animal kingdom. This is the 'discipline of natural consequences', advocated by Rousseau and Spencer. But it remains the lowest level. Found in the adult, for example, it would reveal a complete lack of any sense of responsibility, of duty, of ideals, or of character. In short, it would indicate moral immaturity. Such a person would be a moral child.

The terms 'prudential' and 'expedient' have been used to describe such a level of morality. But both are ambiguous and therefore unsatisfactory. 'Prudential' still has lingering overtones of the admirable cardinal virtue of prudence, and it is therefore inappropriate to associate it with this lowest level. Similarly, 'expedient' is a term that may be used by a highly moral person – in holding, for example, with Paul, that there are perfectly legitimate actions which, for the sake of others, it may not be expedient to practise.

1 Anomy and Heteronomy

We may notice, before going further, a link between anomy and heteronomy. The controls of the former are pain and pleasure; the controls of the latter are punishment and reward. The former is the 'discipline of natural consequences'; the latter is the discipline of artificial consequences, in the sense of its being imposed by adults. Punishment has links with pain, and reward with pleasure.

It is, therefore, not always easy to distinguish between these two levels of moral judgement in the responses of younger children. Indeed, given our definition of stages, we should expect mixed responses at all ages – and, of course, in different situations – although we would expect, and find, greater stability and generality with moral development.

In the cheating situation, for example, three boys of 7 years think it wrong because: 'You only get caught'; 'He might have the wrong answers'; 'You always get it wrong.' But the same boys, asked if cheating would be all right if undetected, reply: 'Yes. It would help me get a star'; 'Yes. He wouldn't be seen'; 'Yes. Nobody would know.' Similarly, a girl of 7 years thinks cheating wrong 'because you only get caught'; but, if undetected, 'you wouldn't get into trouble and it wouldn't matter'.

Stealing is a far more serious matter to children of all ages than the rather artificial 'crime' of cheating. A boy of 7 years, asked if the child will steal from the open bag in the cloakroom, replies: 'Yes. He wants it. His Mum wouldn't buy him one. He'd feel happy.' Similarly a girl of the same age thinks that 'she'd be afraid of being found out. But she'd be happy because she got what she wanted.'

2 Situational Differences

As already observed, we inevitably find mixed responses in the same child and in terms of different facets of the same situation. That is to

say, in other words, that stages or levels of moral judgement overlap;
and thus, in terms of scoring responses, it was vital to use half-scores.
The four levels of judgement were scored in an ascending scale:
anomy, 1; heteronomy, 2; socionomy, 3; autonomy, 4. Where, therefore, we find elements of both anomy and heteronomy in the same
subject's responses we award a half-score for each, making a total of
$1\frac{1}{2}$. In seeking to trace development, therefore, our concern is with
total responses, and not with individuals, within each age group.

At 7 years we find 20% of the total of boys' responses and 21% of
the girls' responses, on the pre-moral level, in terms of all four
situations. The figure for boys is still almost identical at 9 and 11
years; while the figure for girls, already diminishing at 9 years, is
reduced to 8% at 11 years. Thereafter this element is minimal in
girls' responses, whereas with boys it is still 10% at 15 years, and 5%
at 17 years. While for both sexes, therefore, the main development is
between 11 and 13 years, this lowest level of moral judgement remains throughout much stronger in boys than in girls.

But, as always, the situational element is a vital concern. Naturally,
we find pre-moral judgements strongest in the cheating situation,
given the artificality of cheating as an 'evil' to children. They make
up 33% of the total responses of the 7-year age-group and 23% at 11
years, being thereafter minimal in girls' responses and residual in
boys' responses.

Conversely, the Value of Life Test, raising the most serious issue of
life and death, produces but the barest evidence of this level, and that
is so at all ages. In this situation, of course, the play of sympathy,
born of the process of identification, is apparent already in our
youngest age-group.

In the stealing situation, there is no difference between boys and
girls at both 7 and 9 years, with 20% of responses indicating this
level in each sex and age group. But the reduction in this figure
shown by girls at 11 years is not reached by boys until 13 years. The
temptation to steal, if not strong, remains a typically masculine
problem.

The lying situation produces most interesting evidence of the sex
differences that we shall observe throughout. At 7 years, 20% of the
total responses of both boys and girls are at this pre-moral level. The
figure remains the same for boys until 11 years, only diminishing to
13 years and to 5% at 17 years. But this reduction to 5% is already
achieved by girls of 9 years. Here we see the far greater natural

sensitivity of girls to personal relationships, for lying strikes at the heart of all truly personal communion.

3 Anomy as a Level of Judgement

We would naturally expect this pre-moral level of judgement to be most apparent in the immature age-groups. We would not expect it after the climacteric development between 11 and 13 years. But we do find it, if in boys rather than in girls. We may illustrate from the stealing situation. An extreme case is a boy of 15 years: 'If a boy leaves a bag open he deserves to have it stolen. If it's money the boy is taking, he will feel happy. Money is just about everything.' But he is not alone. Another boy of 15 years judges: 'He'd be pleased, if it was valuable and he wasn't caught.' And a boy of 17 years says: 'He'd take something and feel good. He wouldn't care.'

Similarly, in response to the lying situation, a 13-year-old boy says: 'I don't think it's wrong, not if you can get away with it.' At 17 years, three boys still hold that lying is all right if undetected.

Such responses are naturally few in the maturer age-groups. They might, of course, be placed in a more sophisticated category of 'expediency'. But their most significant characteristic is, surely, that the only controls they know are pain and pleasure.

The lowest stage in moral development thus remains as a level of moral judgement at maturer ages, if in boys rather than in girls, and if minimal.

4 Absence of Conscience

All such pre-moral judgements are characterised by the absence of evidence of interiorised moral sentiments. We find no such evidence in the 7-year age-group. They are overwhelmingly rooted in heteronomy: and dominated at best, therefore, by fear of detection and consequent punishment.

Such fear, with its associated anxiety, may be regarded as the initial factor in the growth of conscience (e.g. Stephenson, 1966). Here, then, would be the first roots of interiorised morality; and hence the legitimacy of describing this as the 'pre-moral' stage. When we meet such judgements in maturing adolescents, however, there is minimal evidence of fear – and small hope, we might conclude, of maturing conscience.

3
External Morality

Heteronomy

Kant introduced the Greek terms 'heteronomy' and 'autonomy' in order to define the profound distinction between a morality imposed from without and a morality freely accepted and stemming, therefore, from within. Heteronomy is the constraint imposed upon the individual by others, a control backed by force of one kind or another. The rules imposed are obeyed because they have authority behind them.

1 *Its Paradoxical Characteristics*

Heteronomy is, therefore, an external morality. Its sanctions are rewards and punishments. Its purpose may be broadly defined as to train the child in the control of natural impulses. 'Fear being the great inhibitor of action', the 'fear of punishment can secure this control' both effectively and early. Such an imposed morality is, therefore, essential for the child, strengthening and augmenting the natural processes within the child that we have previously observed. But the morality of heteronomy remains, essentially, 'the conduct of a slave' (McDougall op. cit., 162).

Here, then, we observe the two essential, if paradoxical, characteristics of, heteronomy. First, it is absolutely vital for the child to have the external morality of heteronomy imposed upon him if he is to develop morally. He must serve his moral apprenticeship before he can work on his own. He must learn to control natural impulses, and must therefore be disciplined by others, if he is to have any hope of achieving self-discipline.

But, secondly, the morality of heteronomy is external, forced, servile. While it is legal, it is – in the strict sense of the word –

immoral. For it goes against the essential characteristic of genuine morality – that it must be the free expression of a free individual.

2 Heteronomy a Means to an End

How, then, are we to resolve this paradox? We resolve it by realising that heteronomy is a means to an end – never an end in itself. It is the apprenticeship whose whole purpose is to produce the master-craftsman. It is the imposition of discipline from without in order that self-discipline may be developed within. It is, in short, the resolution of the paradoxical relationship between discipline and freedom. There can be no true freedom without discipline, for there is all the difference in the world between freedom and licence. No one is free to drive until he has disciplined himself in the rules of the road, control of his vehicle, and mastery over himself and his impulses. In every sphere of life discipline is the prerequisite of freedom.

Heteronomy is imposed upon the child by adults – chiefly parents and teachers. They know well enough that it is essential. But their great temptation is to become so accustomed to it as, in effect, to make it an end in itself. It makes life, after all, so much easier. It becomes progressively harder to give up the reins controlling the child. Adults are rightly authoritative in imposing heteronomy, provided that they not only make rules reasonable, but also, so far as possible, show the reasonableness of the rules they impose. But they are wrongly authoritarian; for this is to treat the child as an unthinking, unfeeling slave who must learn to obey his master's commands, regardless of whether he understands or accepts them. If *laissez faire* breeds frustration and uncertainty, authoritarianism breeds resentment and, ultimately, rejection. Only a true democracy, with its basic principle of respect for the individual, can make heteronomy wholesome and effective in relationships between persons.

3 Its Dangers as an End in Itself

When heteronomy becomes, in practice, an end in itself, the child's moral growth is stunted and development held back. He is cemented in a servile state. Instead of being helped onwards to man's moral estate, he is forced to remain a perpetual child, a moral Peter Pan. In times when authoritarianism held sway, such unthinking obedience could be imposed; it was not for the child to reason why, simply to obey. But this is no longer tolerated – and not least as the result of the modern development of an educational service which, for all its faults, teaches the young to think for themselves – and therefore to ask the reason why. It is no longer enough to cite an authority, whether divine or human, for moral principles. A moral code must be seen to be reasonable, and it is in its reasonableness that its authority must lie.

A reasonable heteronomy will be characterised by the giving of responsibility, according to the child's ability to use it – though here, too, the authoritarian may well be inclined to underestimate that ability. A responsible human being can only develop through the practice of responsibility. The goal of heteronomy is the free, morally responsible individual. It is never an end in itself.

4 Heteronomy as a Level of Judgement

Such a view of heteronomy may well seem idealistic and irrelevant in the cold light of contemporary society, and not least of contemporary youth. The majority do not think out their moral principles, but, rather, absorb them unthinkingly from their social environment or group. There is, moreover, an essential irrationality in every human being. And would any organised human society be possible without the heteronomy of the law, backed ultimately by sanctions of force?

It remains true that a wholly heteronomous environment must produce individuals who, if they do not rebel, can only have a heteronomous morality. Never having been allowed to develop an inner morality, they remain dependent upon external sanctions – the only controls they know. For a boy brought up in such an environment, a career in the army, in a context of externally imposed discipline, might well be congenial. Some remain heteronomous all their days – controlled, that is, deterred, by fear of the law and of punishment. A religion, too, may be heteronomous, requiring obedience from its adherents to set rules of belief and practice, with the force of religious sanctions behind them. Some will prefer the security of such a typically Catholic expression of religion to the burden of the individual Protestant conscience.

In any sphere of life, heteronomy is unlikely to promote a reasoned code. Heteronomy breeds heteronomy. 'Father's the one I'd get the biggest walloping from,' says a girl of 17 years; 'Mother is more authoritarian,' says a boy of the same age. Small hope here, one might think, of the free development of an inner, reasoned moral code.

It is also true that adults imposing heteronomy, rather than developing a personal relationship of trust, tend to defeat their own ends. Rigid, if not ruthless, discipline may well breed the very immorality that it fights so fiercely. A boy of 17 years commented thus on the lying situation: 'If his father was vicious, he would lie. If his father was understanding, he'd tell the truth, and get advice about what to do for the best.' Hence the insight revealed by a boy of 13 years: 'Father would punish me more, so I'd feel more conscience about lying to my mother.'

The fact remains, however, that we all need heteronomy in some measure, and in some situations, all our lives. If, yet again, we illustrate from driving, the law imposing breathalyser tests is yet another example of the fact that neither reason nor concern for others are strong enough to control the moral behaviour of adults at all times and in all situations. Some think of such laws as illegally restricting personal freedom. In fact, they legally preserve and defend it; for the individual may now drive free from the danger of drunken drivers. Such heteronomy is not the same in kind as the heteronomy imposed on the child by the authoritarian teacher or parent, for the adult is free to act on a higher level.

Whether because of our human weakness, or because of strictly heteronomous upbringing, or of both, we all continue to need in some measure the sanctions of heteronomy – the carrot of reward and the stick of punishment. In short, heteronomy is not only a stage in the moral growth of the child: it remains a level of judgement throughout life, to a lesser or greater degree.

Piaget's Two Moralities of the Child

While Piaget borrowed the term 'heteronomy' from Kant, he did not also take over the philosopher's conviction that heteronomy is an essential apprenticeship in the moral craft.

1 Constraint and Co-operation

Piaget's thesis is that there are only two well-defined, starkly contrasted moralities in the experience of the child. The first is heteronomy, the morality of adult constraint, dominant until the age of 7 or 8 years. Here the unilateral respect of the child for the adult produces a morality of obedience and duty. The child, held fast in the straitjacket of heteronomy, has no possibility of moral development.

The morality of constraint is succeeded by the morality of co-operation – at first with other children and later, possibly, with adults. It is this second morality that is the seed-bed of moral development. Through free, reciprocal relationships with his peers, the child develops a morality of mutual respect. To be good is no longer to be obedient; it is to be fair. But through the very experience of reciprocity the child comes to realise that strict fairness is not enough. Motives, relationships, needs and obligations must all be taken into account. Thus reciprocity develops dynamically towards the highest level of autonomy – towards an interiorised morality of goodwill, understanding, forgiveness and love.

Thus Piaget holds that moral development comes from within, not from without – from the child's own inner and automatic processes, not from the heteronomy imposed by adults. Far from assisting the growth of moral concepts heteronomy prevents it. The influence of adults is almost entirely harmful. We can sympathise with such a view when we witness, as Piaget did, the forced imposition of irrational rules by inconsistent and authoritarian adults. But it is quite another thing to elevate such experiences into a universal theory of child development.

2 The Results of Heteronomy

Piaget's theory analyses the subtle effects of heteronomy. First, adult constraint reinforces the child's innate egocentricity to produce 'moral realism'. Adult commands are 'reified', projected into sacred absolutes. 'You *should* get punished,' insists a boy of 9 years, even if the offence against the sacred, adult rule is undetected. Another of the same age is no less vehement: 'No. Even if no one knew it's wrong. It's wicked to tell lies. I would go to bed early to punish myself.' Goodness lies in strict obedience.

Such obedience is to the letter of the law, not to its spirit. What small awareness the child may have of motivation will be suppressed by the power of adult constraint. Responsibility is therefore objective, not subjective. That is, actions are to be judged by their strict correspondence to adult commands, not by the motives behind them. It is more heinous to break twenty cups by accident than to break one in the course of deliberate wrongdoing. The unthinking reaction of an exasperated mother to such an accident may well promote such an idea.

Punishment, of course, is the criterion of wrongdoing. A girl of 7 years gives a stark definition of the offence of lying: 'It's very rude. You get smacked.' But would it be all right if no one knew? 'Yes. You don't get smacked.' It follows that punishment expiates the crime, in the crude justice of heteronomy. Moreover, even nature is allied with the adult in the punishment of wrongdoing. Thus, a boy of 9 years envisages 'an act of God' as punishment for lying: 'Its evil. The Devil tells lies, and God and Jesus doesn't. He might give you chickenpox and make you stay in bed.' And if the lie were unknown, would it be all right? 'Yes. But you *can* be caught because God knows, and He might put it into somebody else's mind.' In this example of such 'immanent justice', both the natural and the supernatural combine to punish.

3 Criticism of Piaget's Theory

It is not our present concern to analyse in detail the defects in Piaget's theory of the two moralities of the child. We shall return later to his high concept of reciprocity. Our concern here is with his blanket condemnation of heteronomy. He utterly rejects the truth summed up in Allport's expressive phrase: 'A "must" conscience precedes an "ought" conscience.'

The examples quoted from our own subjects show that such ideas as those condemned by Piaget are to be found in, probably, most children at this stage of development, if not also in some adults. They are the child's natural interpretation of rules imposed by authority and reinforced by punishment and reward. But Piaget is illogical here. On the one hand, as he says, morality only arises and develops through social living; anomy, the complete absence of moral rule, is only adequate for the solitary. The child, therefore, can only become a human being through socialisation. He must, then, learn social behaviour from adults. But, on the other hand, he is egocentric – and no one has given a more detailed picture of the young child's ego-centricity than Piaget. The child can, therefore, only interpret what he learns within his own natural and narrow limits. Even if his relationships with adults were democratic, rather than authoritarian, there is still much to be learnt that is alien and antipathetic; and much that cannot be reasoned.

We find ample evidence of the external morality of heteronomy in younger children. But we shall also find, later, evidence no less strong that the autonomy of internalised morality stems from heteronomy.
c

Co-operation with peers certainly promotes development towards autonomy. But *both* moralities of the child are necessary for its achievement. Maturing subjects of 17 years are in no doubt about this when they define conscience. It 'comes from society'; 'You'd have no conscience without other people.' But it is not an automatic growth: 'Some people seem not to have one.' Autonomous conscience is, in short, 'the idea of right and wrong put into you by parents and teachers'.

Heteronomy as the Child Conceives It

When concepts begin to develop, at about 7 years, the nature of heteronomy is clearly revealed in children's responses. First, it consists of rules laid down by various authorities, and these adult sources of rules are common to all situations, with varying emphasis. In the matter of stealing, for example, the police are strongly emphasised. Secondly, the sanctions imposed are the negative control of punishment and the positive control of reward. Here, too, there is varying emphasis upon the one or the other. In saving life or returning money found in the street, for example, there is strong hope of reward. In the matter of cheating or of lying, on the other hand, punishment is the operative sanction. Thirdly, the yard-stick of wrongdoing is punishment. Where there is no punishment, therefore, there can be no offence; the one defines the other.

Such emphasis upon punishment is characteristic of raw heteronomy in its most primitive form. The rules thus enforced are no part of the child; he obeys from fear of punishment. It is a sanction hardly distinguishable from the pain sanction of pre-morality. Indeed, the child, at this stage, is essentially anomous, since the rules are no part of him. Piaget, with his massive emphasis upon heteronomy, insists that this phase is crude heteronomy and is not to be defined as even relatively amoral. The distinction, if it exists, is subtle and scarcely more than a matter of viewpoint. Moreover, as we shall see, there is development within the heteronomous stage, as Piaget himself recognises; and in its first crude phase, as we might well expect, it is scarcely differentiated in quality from pre-morality.

I The Negative Control of Punishment

Such crude heteronomy is characteristic of children of 7 years. Lying, for example, is wrong because 'Miss might find out'; or 'His mum would send him to bed'. But it is perfectly all right if undetected; 'nobody would know', is the constant refrain. Cheating, similarly, is wrong because 'you only get caught'; and it too is all right if un-detected because 'you wouldn't get into trouble and it wouldn't matter'. Stealing is, of course, more serious, for the offence is very likely to be found out sooner or later. But the sanction remains the same. 'Teacher says you musn't'; 'He'll be sorry. His Mummy might find out'; 'He'd be sent to prison if he's found out.' Nor is it so easy to dismiss theft, even if it is undetected. A cheerfully frank boy defines stealing as wrong because 'he'll get caught'; but, when asked if it is all right to keep a purse found in the street, he continues: 'No, But I have kept some money I found.'

The feeling tone accompanying such responses, as we observed in discussion of pre-morality, is, at most, that of fear: 'He'd be afraid of being smacked. His face would go red.' But when such responses are found in older age-groups the element of fear rapidly disappears. A boy of 9 years thinks lying wrong because 'you always get found out in the end'; and that if it were not punished there would be no offence: 'I'd just forget about it.' A boy of 13 years judges lies to be all right if unpunished, because 'there are no consequences, you haven't of-fended anyone'. A girl of 17 years, similarly lacking in moral insight, also affirms that lies would be all right if unpunished, because 'wrong is what society punishes'.

When we find such responses in immature children of 7 years, accompanied by overtones of fear, we may see them as on the border-line between pre-morality and raw heteronomy. But, yet again, the sole definition of a moral offence as that which is punished survives, in some individuals, into maturer age, without the aura of fear. It thus becomes a level of judgement, fixated at the level of a morally im-mature child.

2 *The Positive Control of Reward*

It is the drowning test, starkly involved with the issue of life and death, that brings out most strongly the positive control of reward in the heteronomous stage. It, too, is found most strongly in children of 7 years. Moreover, there is also no exact borderline to be distinguished between the pleasure sanction of pre-morality and the reward sanction of heteronomy: 'The boy's Mummy might give him some money.'

The incentive of reward is found in a number of responses: 'You get a reward and become famous'; 'You get a medal for being brave'; 'She would get her name in the papers and be famous'; 'She would get a medal and her friends would cheer her – she would like that.' Hope of reward is still present at 9 years, though much less prominently. A characteristically male response at this age is: 'It would be the right thing to do. He'd get a reward. He'd be a good boy. He'd show off his life-saving.'

In the stealing situation, too, there is natural emphasis upon the hope of reward. It is strong at 7 years. We see here, as always, the complexity of moral motivation; it is by no means always what it seems. Thus, a boy of 7 would hand in a found purse to Teacher; but such apparently strict honesty is, in fact, motivated by the conviction that 'he'd get a team point'. A girl of 9 years will take a found purse to the police, whereupon 'there might be a reward'. Another girl of the same age would act similarly, but with the strong conviction that 'she'll get it back in the end'.

Hope of reward sometimes mingles with fear of trouble. Thus a boy of 9 years says: 'The police would blame him if he didn't help. He was the only person around. He might get a reward.' Another boy of 9 years responds: 'If the boy didn't drown and told the police, he'd get into trouble. He might be rewarded. That's what he's hoping.' Thus, even in a matter of life and death the negative sanction is apparent.

While heteronomy persists in all age-groups, the hope of reward broadly disappears at 11 years. Even where it is found thereafter it is always in association with other and higher levels of judgement. Thus a boy of 13 years provides a typically complex response: 'He might get a reward. He might get into trouble if he didn't help. He'd have it on his conscience.' But it is quite different, as already noted, with the negative sanction of punishment. Fear of pain, of punishment, of trouble – this remains the essential sanction of heteronomy as a level of moral judgement in later years.

3 The Sources of Heteronomy

Since we find heteronomy to be a vital stage in any development towards moral autonomy, it is important to be clear as to the sources of heteronomous rules, however obvious they may seem. For here is the seed-bed of later autonomy.

In the drowning test, the authorities cited are, typically, *parents* – 'Mum and Dad told me that I ought to help people'; *day school* – 'We are taught at school that we must help others'; *Sunday school* – 'You must help people; we learn that at Sunday school.' Religion, as the source of authority, has various expressions, if naïve and verbalistic. Thus: 'God says you should. Jesus might have told him to.' Conversely, a boy of 9 years says: 'If he went away and left him, it would be turning from God and being with the Devil.'

Teacher is, of course, the authority cited in the cheating situation. Characteristic responses at 7 years are: 'It is wrong. Teacher tells us we mustn't ; 'It is forbidden. Teacher tells us not to.' A girl of 9 years emphasises that 'Teacher told them again and again not to cheat'; but cheerfully adds that cheating would be all right if undetected, because 'the other person wouldn't know'. Another girl of 9 years gives a conclusive definition: 'Teacher has said it's wrong, so it's wrong.'

Responses to the stealing situation give further evidence for these as being the sources of heteronomy. Thus: 'God wouldn't like it. We learn at Sunday school that we must not take things'; 'Teacher says you mustn't'; 'He'll be sorry; his Mummy might find out'. Responses citing religion refer typically to the Decalogue. Thus: 'God told people not to steal; it's in the Ten Commandments,' says a boy of 11 years. In another boy of 11 years appears a further, interesting example of immanent justice: 'Jesus might punish him; He might make him trip and lose the money.' But the authority strongly emphasised in this situation is the *police*: 'He'd be sent to prison if he's found out'; 'It's dishonest, because if you're caught you'll be sent to a special school.' While subjects of 7 years would typically hand a found purse to teacher or parent, subsequent age-groups would take it to the police-station. Thus a girl of 9 years says: 'Take it to the police-station. Someone would find out if you'd got it and you would be put in prison.'

Finally, responses to the lying situation cite similar authorities: 'Miss might find out'; 'God wouldn't love you if you told lies'; 'It's against the law'; 'If people find out, they could tell the police'; 'My parents have told me it's wrong'; 'It's naughty. Margaret, my friend, told me.'

The primary sources of heteronomy are, therefore, parents, teachers, Sunday school, police and, rarely cited, friends. Maturing adolescents are quite clear that such were the original sources of their moral concepts. Thus, for example, in terms of stealing, we find such responses from girls of 15 years as: 'My parents told me not to steal'; 'I've been brought up to realise that it is not right to take what doesn't belong to you.' A boy of 17 years comments: 'My parents drummed it into me – it's always wrong for anyone to steal.'

The Development of Heteronomy

1 Qualitative Changes

In the initial phase of raw heteronomy, offences are identified solely by punishment; and there is, therefore, a characteristic emotional overtone of fear. If the authority is removed, or the offence undetected, or punishment not administered, there is no sense of wrongdoing. In this stage, therefore, the controls are like water on a duck's back.

But even within the stage of heteronomy we can observe a development in quality of moral judgement, even if it is not intense. The original rule now becomes universalised. Even money found in the street cannot be kept: 'It's still stealing, no matter what,' says a boy of 9 years.

The acid test of any such development is in responses to the questions: Would it be all right if no one knew? Would it be all right if it was not punished? Raw heteronomy, in its first phase, sees no offence where there is no detection or punishment. Developing heteronomy holds that the offence would remain without either. Piaget recognises this development; but he characteristically insists that it remains essentially heteronomous and that it is a wholly rational process, probably stimulated by co-operation. It is heteronomous because even the universalised rule may still be no part of the child's own autonomous self.

We are here on the borderline between heteronomy and the next stage of socionomy; just as, in considering the first phase of heteronomy, we were on the borderline between pre-morality and raw heteronomy. Piaget recognises no such borderlines; heteronomy is clear-cut at either end. Since heteronomy is, for him, wholly bad in its influence, there can be no question of this universalising of rules developing under the influence of heteronomy.

Such a development may be illustrated, first, by the relationship between offence and punishment. At 7 years, broadly speaking, no punishment means no offence. But at 9 years the offence remains an offence *per se*: 'You *should* get punished'; 'They *should* punish me.' An interesting response from a girl of 9 years is even more developed: 'Lying would be O.K. if my Mum and Dad said so. They always know best. But it's wrong in another way, because I know you shouldn't tell lies.' Another adds that, even without punishment, 'you'd *know* yourself'. A boy of 11 years, invoking the Ten Commandments, insists that, even without punishment, 'you still told a lie, so you should be punished'; and a boy of 13 years responds similarly: 'Teacher would be wrong not to punish.' Even at 9 years other and higher levels of judgement are appearing, within the range of socionomy, and with them a dawning sense of guilt. Here is the overlap between heteronomy and socionomy, the development from the one to the other. The universalising of the rule is an aspect of this development.

We can even see this in the offence of cheating, insignificant as it is to the child. When asked if cheating is all right if undetected, a vacillating boy of 7 years replies: 'I suppose so. No, it's wrong.' At 9 years we find, in answer to the same question, such responses as: 'No. Cheating is like lying, it's wrong'; 'No. Because cheating is wrong anyway'; 'No. She had been told it's wrong'; 'No. You should be punished, then you would stop.' Very human is the boy of 11 years who replies: 'No. But do it, and try to make up your mind not to do it again.' Here, too, other and higher motivating factors are to be found.

Thus the original heteronomous prohibition develops into a universal rule. It becomes a moral imperative. Piaget holds that it remains external to the child; and that it probably develops through co-operation. We find no evidence of co-operation at work here, but, rather, the extension of the rule within the child. Here may be seen one of the links between heteronomy and subsequent development towards the interiorised morality of autonomy.

2 *Quantitative Changes*

A broad picture of the stage of heteronomy can be seen from responses to all four situations from the total sample in each age-group. Heteronomy is strongest at 7 years and 9 years, when it dominates 53% and 54% of responses respectively. At 11 years it has dropped to 42%. With the climacteric development visible at 13 years, it is further reduced to 30%. But, far from disappearing, it is still 21% at 15 years and 12% at 17 years.

In terms of sex differences, an interesting fact is the stronger heteronomy of girls at 9 years. This, it appears, is indicative of their earlier universalising of rules. With that one exception, girls show consistently less heteronomy than boys. This is markedly so from 13 years and upwards. At both 13 and 17 years boys show 10% more heteronomy than girls. Thus boys are much more dependent upon heteronomy. Whether because of the deeper moral insight of girls, or because of the more strongly heteronomous upbringing of boys breeding reliance upon its sanctions, or because of both factors, we see here yet another clear sex difference.

Different situations inevitably produce different levels of heteronomy. Thus it is minimal in a matter of life and death, where the deepest, natural human sentiments are involved. Conversely, we would expect the prohibition of cheating – an offence of no real significance to children – to require strong heteronomy. The cheating situation shows it at both 7 and 9 years; but there is steady decrease from 11 years onwards as other factors enter into judgements upon cheating.

The stealing and lying situations are closely parallel in their evidence of heteronomy. At both 7 and 9 years, and for both sexes, heteronomous responses dominate in both situations, circling around 66%. At 11 years boys show a slight decrease to 60%, and girls a stronger decline to 52%. In the stealing situation, heteronomous judgements decrease steadily in both sexes; but at 17 years the figure is still 28% for boys, as compared with 10% for girls. Evidence from the written tests amply confirmed that stealing is a far greater temptation for boys of all ages than for girls. The problem of lying, too, is far more serious for boys. Even at 15 years, 47% of their responses are still heteronomous. It is not until 17 years that they show a marked decrease to 22%.

3 Heteronomy as a Level of Judgement

Yet again we find that what is a normal stage of child development in moral judgement remains as a firm level of judgement in maturing adolescents. It would be extreme folly to think that heteronomy is a stage of control universally left behind in childhood. For some individuals it remains their sole moral sanction; for others it is necessary in certain situations.

For complete age-groups we find 30%, 21% and 12% of all responses rooted in heteronomy at 13, 15 and 17 years respectively. Boys, of course, are far more dominated by it, with 35%, 26% and 17% of heteronomous responses in these three age-groups. Moreover, we found good reason to assume maturity in moral judgement at 17 years, the evidence showing small likelihood of development thereafter.

Far more refined analysis would be necessary to elucidate the reasons for the abiding need for heteronomy in maturity. Raw human nature might be thought sufficient explanation. But when a girl of 15 years, asked why stealing is wrong, replies that 'you're likely to get caught' and 'my parents would half kill me', one sympathises with Piaget's condemnation of heteronomy. It could be argued that such an individual will respect no other control. But where heteronomy is rigidly imposed as an end in itself it is difficult to see how any other kind of control could possibly develop.

4 Emotional Overtones

Since the dominating control of raw heteronomy is punishment, the natural emotional accompaniment is fear. Such fear of detection and punishment for breaking adult rules is, therefore, strongest at 7 years and 9 years. It may be regarded, as suggested earlier, as the initial factor in the growth of interiorised conscience in normal individuals.

But at 9 years we observe the first glimmerings of a sense of guilt. Thus, in response to the stealing situation, a boy of 9 years speaks of 'feeling guilty', and defines it as 'something that bothers inside when you've done something wrong'. Similarly, in terms of lying, a boy of 9 years holds that a lie would still be wrong if undetected because 'you would know yourself that you'd done wrong'; and a girl thinks the same because 'it starts bothering you after a while'. Another girl of 9 years gives a similar definition: 'No. It's wrong to tell lies and it will be on your mind.'

Such indications of guilt feelings in the 9-year age-group are found in 25% of responses to all four situations. Fear of external sanctions merges into the inner discomfort of guilt. Other terms used to describe it are: guilty, awful, ashamed, dreadful, unhappy, sorry. It is in the 11-year age-group that the term 'conscience' first appears, when 61% of responses reveal interiorised moral feelings expressed in terms of either guilt or conscience. At 13 years there is an increase to

81%, and the term 'conscience' has almost entirely replaced 'guilt'. It is, naturally, the matter of saving life that strongly elicits such intense moral feelings.

We thus see a development from fear to guilt to conscience. The process begins within the stage of heteronomy. There is, of course, an overlap between its later phase and the subsequent stage of socionomy which equates, very broadly, with Piaget's stage of 'co-operation'. He holds that there is no development until heteronomy is out of the way, so that interiorisation only begins when the stage and influence of heteronomy are left behind. He 'hazards the hypothesis' (op. cit., 168) that such interiorisation develops through the influence of co-operation. But our evidence suggests a quite different hypothesis. Rules are first imposed by authority; they are no part of the child. They are then universalised; now they become controls even when detection and punishment are absent. In the first phase the predominant emotion is fear; in the second phase, it is the inner disquiet of guilt, regardless of the offence against the moral rule being unknown by others. And in all this, we observe, there is no reference to co-operation with peers, nor indication of its being an influential factor in the process of development.

The Function of Heteronomy

Such, then, is the function of heteronomy. We see it as the seed-bed of moral autonomy, the apprenticeship that must be served before there can be moral self-mastery. Only discipline imposed from without can lay the foundations of self-discipline within. The process is one of the progressive interiorisation of moral principles imposed by heteronomy. It is, of course, true that free co-operation with others plays its part in that process. But it is not the cause of it.

Heteronomy can, of course, be grossly abused. It is so abused when it becomes an authoritarianism that, imprisoning the child in a strait-jacket of rigidly imposed and ruthlessly enforced external authority, leaves no freedom for development in moral judgement. It is rightly used as a means to an end, giving freedom and responsibility as the child is able to use them. The true function of heteronomy is, therefore, to make itself unnecessary as the child matures. But it remains an absolutely essential phase if there is to be any maturity at all.

4
External-internal Morality

Socionomy

The term 'socionomy' is in keeping with the rest of our terminology to describe the third stage in the development of moral judgement. It covers the very broad area in which judgements are shaped and patterned through relationships with others in society.

External sanctions are still involved. Indeed, in so far as the individual is influenced by the codes of his social groupings, they become of more importance. He conforms to the authority of his peers just as he has learnt to conform to adult authority. He does not want the disapproval of either.

How, then, does socionomy advance beyond heteronomy? The development is within the individual himself. The very fact of co-operating with others is evidence of decreasing egocentricity; and that in itself is moral progress. As a result of such co-operation, too, the individual becomes conscious of himself as a member of a group; and this maturing awareness raises issues of responsibility and obligation. Moreover, a sense of self-respect begins to develop; and it tends to replace fear as a key motivating factor in moral conduct.

1 Social Sanctions

The controls of this stage are social praise and social blame. They exert immense power. Indeed, McDougall holds them to be the dominant moral sanctions of the majority of people. He sees, too, a close link between heteronomy and socionomy. The heteronomous voice of adult authority has developed in the child attitudes of respect, submissiveness and receptivity. The powerful voice of public opinion evokes these same ingrained attitudes.

Other factors reinforce the power of social approval and disapproval. Not least is the fear deriving from the earlier childhood dread of punishment. Active sympathy, too, promotes co-operation with others, for the dread of social isolation makes conformity imperative. There are also the altruistic motives that stem from relationships of reciprocal affection with others.

But a morality that is founded solely upon social approval and disapproval has obvious limitations. First, it is essentially egoistic. It can of course, be tinged with altruism; but it is not likely to promote selfless concern for others to any strong degree. Secondly, such sanctions lose their power under two conditions: when there is no danger of being found out in breaking the social code, and similarly when the individual is removed from its influence. Thus, for example, it has been said that the history of prostitution is the story of men away from home. But above all, thirdly, such a morality is limited to the *mores* of the society or to one of its sub-groupings.

We distinguished at the outset between morality defined as conformity to the prevailing social code and morality defined as the pursuit of the good. The purpose of education, in its widest sense, is to socialise the child, moulding him into a conforming member of his group; and this must include conformity to its moral code. In small and static primitive societies such conformity was effectively achieved; all the influences upon the child were at one in inculcating the static moral code. Its weakness, of course, was that it gave no freedom for moral development.

Such rigid conformity to a rigid code can no longer be effectively achieved, least of all in a changing democratic society, and one in which a child may come into contact with any number of varying codes. But there is always an inherent weakness in identifying the moral with the social. Moral progress is made by the individual, autonomous conscience that challenges the prevailing moral code. In such challenges there must be a factor at work beyond society. They stem from the autonomous conscience. Here, indeed, is the essential distinction between socionomy and autonomy. Socionomy relies upon and conforms to the social code. Autonomy neither relies upon it nor necessarily conforms to it.

2 *Inner Sanctions*

Socionomy is, none the less, an essential stage of development if autonomy is to be achieved – even if many become fixated at this level of moral judgement. For it is not simply a stage in which there develops increasing conformity to the external code of the group. There are also dynamic processes at work within the individual.

The sanctions may remain essentially external, as in heteronomy. But we have seen evidence of some inner development even within the stage of heteronomy; and it is such development that is characteristic of socionomy. Awareness of others, relationships with others, some sense of responsibility to others, mutual codes of behaviour with others – these are the hallmarks of socionomy.

Piaget has brilliantly analysed these dynamic processes at work in this 'morality of co-operation' – the second of his 'two moralities of the child'. There is much more at work than a growing conformity to social codes among peers. An individual may, of course, progress no further and remain rooted for life in a tit-for-tat code of behaviour. But he may make such moral progress that the voice of conscience within becomes so powerful as to defy the voice of public opinion without. Such progress is made possible by the processes at work in this stage of socionomy. Piaget sums them up in the term 'reciprocity'.

Reciprocity

I The Meaning of Reciprocity

Reciprocity is defined in the Golden Rule: 'As ye would that men should do to you, do ye also to them likewise' (Luke 6.31). But it is not, of course, limited to Christianity. We find it, whether in its positive or negative form, in every creed and philosophy of man. It is, in fact, the common moral coinage of humanity, a universal principle for human relationship.

But it is, of course, a principle – not a rule as such. It therefore requires interpretation and must be translated into detailed ethical codes. It is no substitute for moral rules, though it should underlie them. In particular, it will remain an irrelevant abstraction to the child unless it is applied to detailed moral situations.

A second defect of reciprocity is that it may be limited in both quality and quantity. It may be mainly motivated by self-interest. 'You help them – they'll help you', as a child puts it. Such calculation is not of the highest moral quality. Moreover, such enlightened self-interest may not go very far. It certainly makes no such demands as the call to self-giving love, to go the extra mile that active benevolence gladly undertakes.

The range of reciprocity, thirdly, is vast. Some children quote approvingly the iron law of 'eye for eye, tooth for tooth'. Others, at the other extreme, say that 'we should all love one another'. Reciprocity thus comes in danger of being a blanket term. Piaget recognises this breadth of reciprocity. It begins with strict mathematical vengeance, but develops of itself, he holds, into a reciprocity of generosity, benevolence and love. For Piaget, therefore, autonomy grows out of reciprocity.

2 Evidence for Reciprocity

It is the stark issue of life and death, in the Drowning Test, that gives us our main evidence for reciprocity. 76% of all such responses were evoked by it, as compared with 20% from the Stealing Test, and but 4% from the Cheating and Lying Tests combined. Thus reciprocity is only an overwhelming factor in judgements on the value of life.

By contrast, the citations of conscience as the motivating factor were almost double those of reciprocity. Of such conscience responses, 45% were evoked by the Value of Life Test, 31% from the stealing situation, 15% from the Lying Test, and even 9% from the Cheating Test. Thus, while all four situations evoke conscience to a lesser or greater degree, only the Drowning Test substantially involves reciprocity. It does not appear, therefore, that autonomy is universally born of reciprocity, as Piaget theorises.

In particular, Piaget holds that autonomy makes its first appearance in the lying situation. The child realises that telling the truth is essential to personal relationships of free co-operation; so that reciprocity is, again, the causative factor. The lying test, however, produced but 3% of all our responses motivated by considerations of strict reciprocity. And further, even when specifically asked about lying on behalf of friends, only 4% of all responses cited reciprocity. Reciprocity, it appears, does not breed autonomy in terms of truthtelling. What then does? We see, rather, the deepening interiorisation of the prohibition of lying first laid down by heteronomy, and consequently extended and universalised.

Certainly many children come to realise that lying breaks trust. But even this conviction may well have heteronomous roots. 'My Mummy says that if you tell lies no one will believe you,' says a girl of 7 years. 'You should always tell the truth because Mother and Father don't trust you else,' says a girl of 9 years. Piaget always tosses aside such 'adult sermons', as he terms them. But, while in origin such responses must be parental or pedagogic maxims external to the child, they can and do become part of him. In rejecting all such originally heteronomous shibboleths, Piaget throws out the baby with the bathwater.

3 Sympathy and Reciprocity

The Drowning Test, with its stark issue of life and death, touches upon and evokes the deepest strands of the child's moral potential. It shows that, as Piaget suggests, the sense of reciprocity derives from natural sympathy. Here, as in every aspect of moral judgement, we observe a process of development. Native sympathy merges into a sense of reciprocity; and, in this deepest of all moral situations, reciprocity merges into autonomous conscience.

McDougall holds that the maternal instinct is the ultimate source of all altruism. This is to some extent supported by our finding that 75% of girls of 7 years show sympathy merging into reciprocity, as compared with 53% of boys. Further, 47% of boys of 7 years respond on the levels of anomy and heteronomy, as compared with 25% of the girls. Thus, while any adult would hold it to be 'instinctive' to save life, we see no such innate instinct. Rather do we see sympathy as providing the potential for moral development.

Sympathy is strong in the 7-year age-group. It would be 'unkind' to abandon the child in the water, say many; 'He would feel so sorry for him,' says a boy. A girl, typically more expansive, says, 'She felt sorry for the person in the water and wanted to help. She just wanted to – she's a kind girl.' Even stronger is the response: 'She wants to save her from drowning, even though she doesn't know her.' Such sympathy merges into a sense of reciprocity, even at 7 years. Why should you save life? 'I just think you should. I wouldn't like to drown,' says a boy. 'She thinks how she would feel if she was in the water,' says a girl. Sympathy may thus develop into empathy, through the process of identification.

At 9 years the sense of reciprocity becomes more and more prominent, incorporating waning sympathy. 'You don't want them to die. You don't want to die yourself' is the stout, masculine type of response echoed by other boys. A sense of the value of human life appears, too: 'He'd save him because it's a person.' Girls make similar responses: 'She would want saving herself, if it was her. I wouldn't like to drown myself.' Among girls, too, we find a sense of the value of human life, as compared with that of animals. It is quaintly expressed. 'A girl can be more use than animals', and, in any case, 'an animal has a few more lives'; moreover, 'you can't buy little girls in shops'. At 9 years, too, there is the first appearance of the term 'murder', or the equivalent 'killing', to describe abandoning the drowning child; and a first suggestion that saving life is 'instinctive' in a girl's response that 'it's the only thing any human would do'.

Reciprocity is cited also, if far less strongly, in the stealing situation. One boy of 7 years says: 'I wouldn't like anyone to steal from me.' Four girls of the same age make similar responses, one of them characteristically feminine: 'She wouldn't want anyone to steal from her, and she thinks about the other girl's feelings.' A girl of 9 years judges it wrong to keep a found purse because 'if she lost something she'd want it returned'. Reciprocity is a little stronger at 11 years, seen in such responses as 'I wouldn't like anybody to take mine.' Here, too, we find a rare citation of the Golden Rule: 'No. Take it to the police. You must do as you would be done by.' Reciprocity also lingers on in older age-groups in the stealing situation. But increasingly it is conscience that motivates judgement.

4 Reciprocity and Conscience

Sympathy was thus characteristic of the 7-year age-group in the Value of Life Test – more strongly so in girls than in boys. But it decreases at 9 years with the dramatic rise of the sense of reciprocity – again more strongly apparent in girls than in boys. For total age-groups, the 7% of responses indicating reciprocity at 7 years increases to 48% at 9 years, with a similar 46% at 11 years. Thereafter it fades to 27% at 13 years, with the dramatic rise of responses citing conscience.

A sense of reciprocity thus dominates the 9-year and 11-year age-groups – if only substantially elicited by ultimate concern with life and death. It does remain a factor in the judgements of some older children, but it is massively replaced by conscience. A sense of guilt is evidenced in 25% of the 9-year age-group. At 11 years the actual term 'conscience' makes its first appearance, 38% of the age-group using it, in addition to the additional 23% expressing feelings of guilt. Thus 61% of the 11-year age-group reveal interiorised moral sentiments, increasing to 81% at 13 years, when reciprocity fades.

In short, therefore, reciprocity is replaced by conscience as the dominant motivating factor in moral judgement. Can we, therefore, infer – on the principle *post hoc propter hoc* – that conscience has developed from the sense of reciprocity? Can we, that is, agree with Piaget that 'autonomy appears only with reciprocity' (op.cit., 194) – that reciprocity tends 'of itself', by its own dynamic process, towards autonomous conscience?

We certainly find no evidence for such a theory outside the Value of Life Test. In particular, we find no support for it whatever in the lying situation, where Piaget holds reciprocity to be the 'determining factor of autonomy' (op.cit., 194). Nor do we find any evidence for it in the stealing situation, where responses have strong emotional over-tones – as, indeed, in the lying situation.

There is, moreover, a contrast between the warmth of responses citing conscience and the more chilly, more cognitive responses of rather calculated reciprocity. 'I'd want to be saved if I was him' is of a piece with 'You save them, they'll save you.' Sympathy and a measure of identification are, of course, involved – though almost solely in a life-and-death situation. But the atmosphere of self-interest surrounding reciprocity responses contrasts with the self-guilt of conscience responses.

We must observe, too that strict reciprocity remains a solid factor in moral judgements of older children. Thus, in the Value of Life Test, we find it represented in 27% of all responses at both 13 and 15 years, and still in 17% at 17 years. It thus remains a level of judgement in maturity – although strictly, according to Piaget, it should have developed 'of itself' into autonomy. Moreover, we find reciprocity and conscience cited side by side in older age-groups; and here conscience seems to reinforce reciprocity, not to proceed from it. Thus a boy of 13 years responds: 'You'd want to be saved yourself. He'd save the boy – his conscience would make him.' And again, whereas reciprocity may motivate immediate action and thereafter be forgotten, conscience would keep failure to help on one's mind – 'for the rest of life' say many subjects. A boy of 17 years gives a definitive response: 'He'll jump in and try to save him. He'd have a bad conscience if he didn't, thinking about it all the time. You've only got one life. If you don't help others, others won't help you.'

To sum up, therefore, we cannot agree with Piaget that autonomous conscience is the automatic fruit of a sense of reciprocity. We see a different process at work. Rules are laid down by, and attitudes

D

observed in, respected adults. They are progressively extended and interiorised through the process of identification. Thus interiorised moral feelings of guilt arise when they are broken; and such sense of guilt develops into the autonomy we call 'conscience'. Hence the strongly orectic nature of responses citing conscience, as contrasted with those based on a sense of reciprocity. Autonomy, we conclude, is born of heteronomy – not of reciprocity.

The Sense of Justice

We have seen that the sense of reciprocity dominates children at 9 and 11 years of age. Now reciprocity, as defined universally in the Golden Rule, lays down the basic principle of justice: ... 'everyone's conduct must be judged by the same standards . . . what is right or wrong for one person must be right or wrong for any similar person in similar circumstances' (Singer, 1963). Hence such responses to the Value of Life Test as: 'He has as much right to live as I have . . . I'd want to be saved if I was in his position.'

But when the sense of reciprocity first develops it is naturally immature, crude and raw. It simply sticks to the basic principle, without any such mature refinements as taking motives and circumstances into account. All must be judged by the same strict yardstick; all must be treated exactly alike. The slightest deviation elicits the incessant parrot-cry of reciprocity, 'It's not fair.' In the stage of heteronomy, to be good was to be obedient. In the stage of socionomy, to be good is to be fair.

1 The Situations

The drowning situation is far too serious and intense for nice calculations of fairness – as, from another viewpoint, is the stealing situation. Lying, again, falls within the intense context of personal relationships, and gives only small scope for considerations of fairness. A boy of 9 years holds that lying 'is not fair on your friends'. A girl of 11 years responds: 'You could get others into trouble. It's not fair to do this by telling lies.' A boy of 13 years judges that lying 'is not fair to the other person'. Even at 17 years one or two boys make similar judgements. Such responses are, however, minimal in the intimacy of personal relationships.

But it is in the cheating situation that this dawning sense of justice really comes into its own as the operative factor in judgements. Here, yet again, we see the importance of the situational element; and, therefore, the importance of securing children's judgements upon a variety of situations. The value of including a cheating situation – even if this is no real crime to children – also becomes apparent. Cheating, of course, becomes a crime to the strict principle of reciprocity. But it is a crime against peers – not against authority as such. Here, therefore, is fertile ground for securing judgements upon fairness. To ensure fully representative responses, we used two cheating situations – the heteronomous classroom and free co-operation in playing games.

2 *It's not Fair*

Only one child of 7 years sees that cheating in the classroom is 'unfair', adding the 'adult sermon': 'You never learn that way.' It is, naturally, in the free co-operation of games that children first realise the strict justice of reciprocity. Thus at 7 years we find a few such responses: 'It is not fair to the others' or the variant, 'It would be very unfair to the others.'

At 9 years the dramatic increase in the sense of reciprocity is typified by the realisation that cheating is unfair in the classroom situation, not simply at games. Thus 'It wouldn't be fair on the rest of the class'; 'It's not fair, getting rewarded for somebody else's work'; 'It wouldn't be fair on the boy who is working honestly.' A few girls make similar responses.

At 11 years a boy responds: 'It's not really fair. It takes away the chance of the others to do well'; and similarly a girl answers: 'It's not a fair way to get the answers. Why should *she* do it the easy way?'

The same type of response is still found at 13 years. Cheating is 'unfair to the others; you're stealing off them'. At games it is 'unfair to the other person or team'; moreover, 'it's not using your own skill; it's not fair'.

There are, of course, other factors at work in the cheating situation. Anomy is strong in judgements on so artificial a 'crime'; and hence the strong need of heteronomy. Moreover, as we shall see, the purely social sanction of being branded a cheat is a powerful deterrent. Above all, growing intelligence realises the stupidity of cheating: 'You only cheat yourself'. Nor, indeed, was conscience entirely irrelevant to the matter of cheating, this situation producing 9% of all responses citing conscience.

3 Fairness between Children

One of our written tests was wholly concerned with analysing children's justice concepts. In particular, it examined the conviction of Piaget that reciprocity increases with age. Durkin, replicating Piaget's work, had already found the contrary. One of the stories we used dealt specifically with free relationships between peers. Children vociferously denounce any unfairness – that is, lack of strict reciprocity – when others gain by it. Are they so dominated by reciprocity in dealings among themselves?

The story we used ran: 'Joan sat behind Sheila at school. One day, Joan found that she had left her ruler at home. She asked Sheila if she could borrow hers. Sheila would not lend it to her. A day or so later, Sheila left her rubber at home. She turned round and asked Joan if she could borrow hers. Do you think Joan would lend it to her? Why do you think that?'

Here we were entirely concerned with the free interplay of practical justice between themselves. Nothing opened up more clearly the labyrinth of reciprocity. Far from being a simple, clear-cut entity, it ranges with infinite complexity from the tit-for-tat of 'one bad turn deserves another', through the more enlightened 'two wrongs don't make a right', to the disinterested altruism of forgiveness and bene-volence. The dismal judgement, 'No. You wouldn't, so I won't,' is justified on the basis of 'an eye for an eye' which some quote as melancholy proof of knowledge of the Christian Scriptures.

At both 9 and 11 years, 90% of responses are rooted in such reci-procity. But yet again the climacteric development revealed at 13 years reduces such responses to 69%. There is a parallel rise in higher responses from 9% at 11 years to 31% at 13 years. Here again we see reciprocity dominant at 9 and 11 years, but thereafter solidly decreas-ing. But it by no means disappears.

We must disagree with Piaget's twin assertions – that reciprocity increases with age, and that it breeds altruistic autonomy. At 17 years we find 63% of all subjects rigidly cemented in such reciprocity, the boys as usual predominating, as compared with 25% showing pure altruism.

It would indeed be pleasant to be able to share Piaget's optimism. But reciprocity remains a solid, and somewhat harsh, level of moral judgement in maturity. What was an appropriate stage in late child-hood becomes an immature level in adulthood. Had Piaget not ended his testing at about the age of 12 years he must surely have come to see the fallacy of the theories be propounds.

Social Conformity

We said initially that the sanctions of the stage of socionomy are social praise and social blame. We have been concerned thus far with the dynamic development going on within the child. What is the place of social praise and blame in this process?

Late childhood is a stage of social conformity. The child now becomes conscious of himself as a member of a group. The individuality of his earlier egocentricity is replaced by sociability. He naturally desires the company of his peers; and, as Piaget notes, the worst punishment of reciprocity is banishment from the group. Such isolation – indeed, any form of 'being different' – is anathema at this stage. Groups are the typical expression of such sociability; but, as research has clearly shown, they are very different in nature from the tight-knit 'gangs' of adolescence. Such a group is the natural expression of this clan stage of 'the primitive man'.

The strong impulse of this stage is therefore to conform to the group. Nor is this only outward conformity – in dress and appearance, for example. It is a conscious concern to be in all respects one of the group, and to act as the others do. Hence the strength of the sanctions of social praise and blame.

1 Saving Life

The drowning scene, once again, is far too intense to be a matter of social conformity. A rare citation is that of a boy of 15 years: 'People would think bad about you, if you let him drown,' but his full response refers in addition to both reciprocity and conscience. An immature response from a boy of the same age is limited to this level: 'His friends would talk about him if he didn't. They'd say he should have saved him. They'd have thought he killed the boy.' Similarly, an immature boy of 17 years responds: 'He'd be afraid of what people would say.'

2 Cheating

In the cheating situation, too, the rabid demand of reciprocity for strict equality leaves little room for the play of social sanctions, though they are involved to a degree. Of cheating at a game, one boy of 11 years says: 'He might if it's hard. He wouldn't if it's easy. The other boys might walk off and leave him'; and another of the same age: 'No. More people are watching him. His friends will call him a cheat and a fouler and throw him out of the team.' Only one refers to the classroom situation: 'No, nobody likes to be called a cheat – the other children would get to know.'

A girl of 13 years thinks cheating wrong, even if undetected by the teacher, 'because the other girls would see you'; but her main motive is that 'you would feel guilty about it'. A girl of 17 years responds: 'People can always see it in your face. They won't like you in the end for it'; and another girl of the same age: 'You don't gain anything. Your friends despise you.'

Social sanctions do not, therefore, operate at any strength in the cheating situation. Continuing heteronomy, strict equality – above all, increasing realisation of the stupidity of cheating ('You only cheat yourself'), even conscience – these motivations are too strong for social praise and blame to be significant controls.

3 Stealing

The stealing situation, again, is too serious a matter to be controlled to any degree by social sanctions. From 9-year boys come two responses: 'He would be called a thief'; 'People will call him a stealer'; and from a girl of the same age: 'Everyone will call you a thief.'

A girl of 13 years thinks that 'her friends would be upset, and that would make her sorry'. A boy of 15 years responds: 'Your friends would call you a thief.' A boy of 17 years says: 'Stealing is against the law and what people think. They won't trust him.' Another of the same age sums up the matter: 'The opinion of others is only part of it, not the whole reason. It's wrong. It's not yours. It's always wrong to steal. You haven't worked for it.'

4 Lying

The lying situation does give more evidence of social sanctions at work. But the evidence is clouded, as it were, by the increasing realisation that lying breaks trust. It therefore not only negatively tends to harm personal relationships, but may also produce positive dislike. We might therefore see social sanctions at work here. But the two main objections to lying are that it breaks trust, and that it may bring pain or trouble to others. Both these factors are increasingly within the context of developing autonomy. It would, therefore, be incorrect to limit the realisation of breaking trust and hurting others to the level of social sanctions.

Two boys of 9 years are motivated by social sanctions: 'You get a bad name with your friends. You get called a liar'; 'Your friends don't like you.' Four girls of the same age give similar judgements: 'The class will call you a liar'; 'No. Her friends will call her a liar'; 'Nobody will be your friend'; 'You lose all your school friends. People start to dislike you.' Such responses are set in the context of reciprocity, and of the extension of the heteronomous rule against lying into a broad principle. As another boy responds: 'People don't like you. It leads to more lies'; and, even if undetected, a lie is still wrong, for 'it's still lying, anyway'.

At 11 years the dawning realisation both of causing trouble to others and of breaking trust reveal the first glimmerings of autonomous conscience – the term 'conscience' itself now first appearing. Social controls are therefore less apparent, and, moreover, are generally mixed with higher insights. Thus, a boy responds: 'Nobody will believe you. You'll be called a liar.' Similarly, a girl replies: 'No. It would be on your mind. Your friends will call you a liar.' Two other girls, showing the strong feminine sensitivity to social opinion, speak with one voice: 'Your friends won't like you.' A fulsome feminine judgement runs: 'Other people will think what a horrible person you are. You'd know yourself, if you told a lie, and Jesus would know. He doesn't like it – nor would anybody if they *did* find out.'

At 13 years one boy responds: 'You get a bad reputation and lose your friends'; but he adds that 'a bad lie would be on your conscience'. Three girls of the same age are concerned with their good name, with adults as well as with peers: 'My friends would think I'm a liar'; 'It doesn't give you a good name'; 'You wouldn't be trusted afterwards – adults wouldn't respect you if they found out.'

At 15 years four boys are similarly concerned with their good name, but in the context of breaking trust: 'It's deceiving – you lose your friends'; 'People don't like you. Your friends won't believe you in future'; 'You're found out and you get a bad name – you're not trusted'; 'It's misleading and you get others into trouble. It's best to be honest – people think more of you. If you deceive someone who trusted you, you lose their trust.' A girl of 15 years shows that sensitivity to others which lies at the heart of all true morality: 'You give the wrong impression to people by lying. You must always consider other people. No, not because of the impression you would create – you mustn't hurt them.'

From 17-year boys we get the familiar responses:'People don't like you'; 'Your friends won't believe you.' One defines the folly of lying succinctly: 'You lose people's trust and respect'; and another: 'You punish yourself by spoiling relationships.' Similarly, a girl of the same age responds: 'It ruins friendships – you wouldn't like a person who keeps lying.'

The Strength of Social Sanctions

Such is the evidence elicited by our four situations for the strength of the social sanctions of praise and blame as factors in moral judgement. It is not strong, save in the lying situation, and there it is associated increasingly with breaking trust – a deeper, more autonomous insight. We may usefully ask why social controls do not appear more strongly.

1 Serious Situations

First, we had deliberately chosen situations involving the worst evils as defined by children of all ages – save, that is, for cheating, which had its own operational controls. Such situations involve moral issues of the deepest concern and significance to children. They therefore elicit the deepest moral attitudes the child has. Had these situations been more superficial and less intense, they might well have shown far more strongly the social controls of social praise and blame.

In particular, these situations elicited, in varying degrees and in varying aspects, the sense of reciprocity that is bred from social co-operation. Whether in terms of seeing oneself in the distress situation of another, or of a fierce demand for strict fairness, or of evils that break up personal relationships, reciprocity is an inner and dynamic process. It does, of course, involve group standards and social sanctions that must be observed. But, as the sense of mutuality grows within, reliance upon external sanctions must weaken.

2 The Influence of the Situation

We have, secondly, found ample evidence of different motivations for judgement in different situations. Yet again the vital significance of the situational element is apparent.

We may illustrate this forcefully from one of our written tests. Children were asked for judgements upon eight quite different situations. Each produced its own distinct pattern of reponse. In two situations – caring for borrowed books and copying in the classroom – judgement was relatively clear-cut between autonomy and anomy. Heteronomy was the dominant level of judgement in situations involving bullying, swearing, and owning up in the classroom – although the last does become much more a matter of autonomy in the older age-groups. A further situation, involving money found in the street, showed autonomy to be the dominant level of judgement – although sympathy played a large part in such judgements.

Socionomy was the dominant level of judgement in two situations. One concerned honesty in pointing out unearned marks to the teacher. There was a strong swing to autonomy at 17 years, but this may be partly due to the moral pressures of the classroom having been left behind. The other situation concerned sharing sweets, and here judgement was overwhelmingly controlled by social sanctions.

Social controls are therefore operative in one type of moral situation, but by no means in all.

3 Mixed Responses

Ample evidence has also been given, thirdly, of the complexity of moral judgements. Again and again they show mixed motivations. The voice of public opinion, heard in the praising and blaming of the individual by others, is certainly a factor involved in many mixed responses. But a moral judgement is seldom single or unitary, especially where conscience develops as a controlling factor. The more immature the individual, of whatever age, and the weaker his integration, the more diffuse his judgements are. At all ages we find a complexity and growing subtlety in moral judgements that makes any unitary theory, such as that of Piaget, quite inadequate to do justice to them.

Moreover, even when conscience does become operative it varies from one individual to another in both quality and quantity. It may be strong or weak in the areas that it does cover. But, while it may operate strongly in one moral area, it may have no sway whatever in another area. Even when an individual achieves some sort of autonomy, therefore, we can still get mixed responses to different situations.

Social sanctions have an undoubted place in the moral judgements of most, if not all, individuals. That place will vary in different individuals, as well as in different situations. In the classic stage of reciprocity they will be most strongly apparent. They undoubtedly survive, too, as the moral controls of many individuals. But they will often be found mingling with other motivating factors.

Socionomy as a Level of Judgement

It was the stark issue between life and death that gave us our strongest evidence for reciprocity. From it, too, we saw how the native sympathy of 7 years has developed into a strong sense of reciprocity at the classic ages of 9 and 11 years. Thereafter, as autonomous conscience develops, reciprocity decreases by half in this drowning situation. But at 17 years it still dominates 34% of all responses. The figure is still the same in terms of all four situations.

Thus socionomy in its broadest sense remains a strong level of moral judgement in maturity. We include in it not only the specific sanctions of social praise and blame, but also the sense of reciprocity which underlies those sanctions and, indeed, gives them their validity. Such reciprocity varies in quality. But its general tone is of the recognition of mutual obligations, due not only to others, but also to the self. It has therefore a contractual element that lacks the self-giving of altruism. Certainly we find no evidence whatever that, as Piaget theorises, such reciprocity develops into autonomy.

Girls show more socionomy than boys at every age, with a particularly strong development at 15 years, and again at 17 years, that makes the sex difference even more pronounced. But even here girls are in advance of boys, since the latter are far more strongly heteronomous. At all ages we observe the far greater sensitivity of girls to other people and so to personal relationships; and they are, therefore, more sensitive to social sanctions and to the possession of 'a good name'.

While reciprocity does not develop into autonomy, the stage of socionomy is an essential phase of moral development if autonomy is to be achieved. External rules are progressively interiorised and extended into universal principles. They are put into practice in growing co-operation with others, through which develops the conscious awareness of reciprocal relationships, of mutual obligations and of concern for others. The stage is thus set for the autonomy of a wholly internalised morality of self-rule.

5
Internal Morality

Autonomy

The fourth and highest stage in the development of moral judgement is that of autonomy, self-rule, when the rules governing moral behaviour come from within the individual. The controls of the stages of heteronomy and socionomy are from without, although both stages are accompanied by an increasing inner development without which autonomy could not be achieved. In the stage of autonomy the controls are internalised; it is, therefore, to this stage that the term 'moral' applies in all its fullness.

1 Autonomy as the Ideal

We must, however, at once ask whether it is legitimate to hold autonomy to be the ideal of moral progress. Such a conviction may itself be regarded as a subjective value judgement. By no means all human societies have held autonomy to be the moral ideal. Some educationists and some educational institutions, in practice even if not in theory, are dominated by the heteronomy of authoritarianism – as are other social and religious institutions. Many, again, would hold conformity to the social code to be the end of education. Such viewpoints may become even more strongly held in reaction to a society that becomes increasingly fluid and permissive in its morality. But the question remains as to whether merely habitual conformity, however firmly imposed, is adequate to a rapidly changing democratic society in which traditional values are weakened by the impact of new knowledge and new attitudes.

There is a broad distinction to be observed between 'shame' and 'guilt' societies. The sense of guilt dominates those societies in which emphasis is laid upon individual responsibility, accompanied by a sense of sin which deepens personal unworthiness. Autonomous conscience – in the shape of the guilt-ridden super-ego – becomes the supreme value. Such societies are typically those affected by the Protestant Reformation. Morality, in such societies, is inner-directed. In shame societies, by contrast, morality is other-directed. The individual sees himself, not in the light of his own inner conscience, but as he appears in the eyes of others. Shame takes the place of guilt.

Some American thinkers see such 'other-directed' anxiety developing as the moral control in traditionally Protestant societies. In our own society the permissiveness, strongly apparent in elements of the younger generation, may be seen as the lack of a sense of guilt in areas where it was, in the traditional puritan code, the supreme control – notably in sexual relationships. Since, however, conscience can only be derived from society, we may see here the failure of the older generation to inculcate such a sense of guilt. Such a failure must stem from refusal to impose the traditional heteronomy; and here the influence of psychology has been profound. No longer is the natural egocentricity of the child seen as original sin, to be beaten down through repressive conditioning, denial of natural instinctive tendencies and breaking of the will. Every biological constituent of the individual has a purpose; all must be recognised and accepted. From them flow both virtue and vice. For moral maturity, therefore, we must, in the dictum of Hadfield (1964), 'know ourselves, accept ourselves, be ourselves'. Hence the search of the young, characterised by much sincerity, for a new basis for genuine personal relationships.

It remains true, however, that, even without deliberate moral education, the normal child naturally develops a moral self through the process of identification; and hence, among other results, the inner conflict that is so characteristic of man. We find ample evidence of a sense of guilt from our probing of areas of deep moral concern. But we shall also observe the struggle to adapt deep-rooted moral principles to personal relationships in concrete, moral situations.

2 *The Nature of Autonomy*

We have distinguished between the controls of socionomy and autonomy as being, on the one hand, the voice of public opinion and, on the other, the voice of inner conscience. What is the nature of this inner voice? What, in other words, do we mean by autonomy?

McDougall holds moral judgements to be rooted in the emotions, rather than in reason; and of nothing is this more true than of conscience. They are built up, of course, from natural sympathy by the processes of suggestion and, above all, of identification. But they can, and often do, conflict with the individual's concrete, personal and more rational judgements. Hence the irrational guilt that many adults experience; and the suggested need for a master-sentiment around which the individual may be integrated.

Piaget says much of autonomy, but scarcely defines it. His interest is in the travelling rather than in the arriving, in the process rather than in the goal, in the dynamics of developing reciprocity rather than in autonomy. He sees it as being 'independent of all external pressure', and as appearing 'only with reciprocity' which 'tends of itself towards a morality of forgiveness and understanding' (op.cit., 194, 231). Thus, in terms of justice, for example, reciprocity first demands strict equality. But this process develops of itself towards the equity of taking into account such factors as motive, circumstance, relationship and obligation. It thus automatically develops until, ultimately, there is no conflict between justice and universal love. We have already examined this sublimely optimistic theory. It brings us little nearer to an understanding of autonomy. In particular, the growing relativity that Piaget sees to be characteristic of this developing sense of justice may mean no more than moral confusion. We shall observe an alternative process at work.

Autonomy may have various aspects. There is, of course, the emotional autonomy that is the characteristic goal of adolescence seeking to break away from the familial bonds of childhood, the theme of many a myth. There is, again, the autonomy of developing an inner code, a process that involves to a lesser or greater degree conscious criticism of conventions previously unconsciously accepted. This, too, is typical of adolescence when much may be rejected in this process of regrouping moral ideals. A third kind of autonomy is that of freely applying one's own moral principles to particular situations, in terms of actual behaviour; and this will be one of our leading interests.

Autonomy is, therefore, a comprehensive term that needs comprehensive definition. We shall be concerned both to trace the development of the autonomous stage of moral judgement and then to see it in action in the concrete situation.

Conscience

1 The term

The Greek term *syneidesis* comes to us from the Stoics, to whom Paul must have been indebted for it. Its classical meaning was of 'consciousness' – and hence consciousness of past action, of having done wrong, and so feeling guilt. Our term comes from the Latin equivalent, *conscientia,* meaning 'knowledge with another', and so 'knowledge with and within oneself'. Conscience was the inner judge, reviewing past action, and giving judgement of praise or blame.

This theme of self-judgement runs through Greek literature and, even more strongly, through the Jewish Scriptures. The sense of inner conflict that the term expresses is characteristically universal. Some have seen it as a function of the mind, others of the emotions, and others of the will. But, as we have seen, far from being an innate faculty, it is an in-built function of the whole personality; and it is, therefore, a construct of society. As such, of course, it will have limitations both in quality and quantity.

2 The Growth of Conscience

We have seen the first beginnings of conscience to lie in the fear that is the emotional accompaniment of heteronomy; for anxiety must be associated with such fear. Thence develops a sense of guilt, with deepening interiorisation, through the identification of child with parent, and feelings of both love and hate being directed towards the same person. Since the child incorporates the parent within himself, to offend against the parent is to offend against himself. Hence the self-punishment of intro-punitive guilt, as contrasted with the fierce condemnation of others that is projected extra-punitive guilt. Thence develops interiorised conscience.

Thus, external controls give way to internal controls. 'I must' gives way to 'I ought'. Fear gives way to self-respect. External discipline gives way to self-discipline. Convention gives way to conviction. The voice of public opinion gives way to the voice of conscience. Such is developed autonomy. But by no means all achieve it, and few achieve it over all areas of moral concern.

3 The Super-ego

The negative aspect of conscience is familiar to us from Freud as the 'super-ego'. It is symbolised, in the colloquial picture, as the old lady upstairs, banging fiercely on the floor whenever the ego is indulging in what, to her, is illicit pleasure. Better still, perhaps, is the primitive image of the pointed stone in the breast, twisting and wounding when wrong has been done.

The super-ego has a double function, both characteristically negative. Unconsciously, it represses intolerable desires and experiences. Consciously, it is the burden of guilt that is born of identifications in early childhood, of aggression which had to be directed inwards upon impulses threatening adult love, and of heteronomous precepts that have become interiorised.

This wholly negative aspect of the moral self would be the definition of conscience given by most adults – as, indeed, by most children, once they become conscious of it. For the vast majority it is the guiding moral control. 'Always let your conscience be your guide' is a good working principle. To go against the super-ego is certainly to court anxiety and guilt. To have no such control is to be a moral imbecile – a psychopath.

Yet such a moral control has its defects. First, it may be irrational in that it condemns actions that reason judges to be perfectly legitimate. Secondly, it may be unhealthy in its repressive and condemnatory functions, so that the adult may need psychiatric help to resolve a pathological burden of infantile distress. Thirdly, it is ineffective in those moral dilemmas where conscience is divided, and the urgent cry is 'What shall I do?' 'Conscience must always be followed', says the moral theologian. But it cannot be followed when it is divided; and certainly history, and not least that of religion, is appallingly disfigured by the enormities of evil done in the very name of conscience.

4 *The Ego-ideal*

There is, however, a second aspect of conscience, the ego-ideal. It is positive rather than negative: rooted in love rather than in fear. Freud failed to differentiate this positive and creative aspect of the moral self from the negative super-ego; and little is known of its nature and genesis. But Hadfield holds the self-critical function of conscience to be itself a derivative from the ego-ideal. It is, essentially, the picture seen by the child of what he must be to secure the love that is his most vital need. But, unlike the super-ego, it develops and grows consciously as the child builds up his ego-ideals.

The picture of the self has three aspects: the self as inwardly known; the self as seen by others; and the ideal self towards which the individual strives. Adults obviously have great influence upon this self-picture, this positive spur to moral growth – and not least parents and teachers. In the contemporary ferment over educational reorganisation, the comprehensive school is championed as giving equality of opportunity, and the abolition of streaming is advocated, since it condemns the less able child to accept himself as being of lower ability, so removing any incentive to development. But the teacher is of no less importance in the shaping of his ego-ideal. It is this, ultimately, that will dominate the child's motivation, whatever the environmental conditions.

With adolescence comes Piaget's stage of 'formal operations' in conceptual development, so that the child is now able to formulate abstract ideas and ideals. It is with adolescence, too, that moral autonomy develops. New values are developed – and some old, assumed values discarded – in the patterning of the autonomous self. Ego-ideals, therefore are vital concerns in seeking to understand the nature of autonomy.

5 *Conscience and Conditioning*

The currently fashionable behaviourist school of psychology holds that conscience is a conditioned reflex, built up in childhood by punishments following upon offences. Fear of punishment motivates moral learning. Experiments with animals – with which human beings are equated – are held to prove the truth of the all-embracing power of conditioning. Thus, human beings may be catalogued according to their conditionability. At one extreme is the anxious neurotic, and at the other the wholly unconditionable psychopath.

Such a theory has clear similarities with the process of identification and of introjection that we have seen to be at work in the whole process of moral development. Clearly, conditioning is part of the process. But it is by no means the whole story. We have noted the powerful processes of imitation, suggestion, identification and the formation of ego-ideals. We have seen, too, the progressive interiorisation of heteronomous precepts, sanctioned by rewards as well as by punishments. Nor, as we shall see, can we ignore the function of reason in adapting the interiorised moral principle, whatever its source, to the pattern of each subtly different situation.

In short, there is far more to moral development than conditioning. Such a theory, in fact, by blandly assuming that human beings are no more than animals, ignores those very human potentialities that differentiate man from animals. Man is an animal; but he is also a moral animal.

6 *Types of Conscience*

Five character types, characteristic of successive stages of development, are well defined by Peck and Havighurst: 'amoral (infancy); expedient (early childhood); conforming and irrational-conscientious (later childhood); rational-altruistic (adolescent and adulthood)'. The process of development was found to be characterised by increasing interiorisation.

Within this development four types of conscience were found: the harsh negative and repressive conscience that is but the echoing voice of the punitive parent; the passive conscience of conformity to rules; the rigid and dogmatic conscience that is Freud's 'tyrannical neurotic super ego'; and the conscience of 'firmly internalised moral principles which are continually open to rational experimentation' (Peck and Havighurst, 1960, 3, 100 f., 170 f). A varying sense of self was associated with these various types of character and conscience. The ideal is clearly the integration of ego and super-ego in the rational-altruistic type of character.

The Development of Conscience

We recall that responses citing conscience were evoked by all our four tests: the Value of Life Test, 117; the Stealing Test, 80; the Lying Test, 38; the Cheating Test, 22. It is interesting to find that the Stealing Test evoked more such responses from younger children. The Value of Life Test produced more conscience responses from older subjects, and many of these were single citations, in that conscience was not quoted in response to any other situation. Thus, it appears that offences against property are, no doubt heteronomously, of greater concern to younger children; and offences against the person far more significant to older children. Moreover, conscience is not universal in its sway; its writ does not run over every area of moral concern.

E

1 At 7 Years

Children of 7 years are rooted in heteronomy. Fear of detection and consequent punishment are universal, and here we may see the first seeds of conscience. Sympathy is strong, in the matter of life and death; and in a small minority such sympathy borders upon a sense of reciprocity.

2 At 9 Years

It is the stealing situation alone which produces the first evidences of a sense of guilt in boys: 'He'd feel awful. He knows he shouldn't have done it'; 'He'd be afraid. He'd feel guilty. It's when you've done wrong, something that bothers you inside'; 'You'd know yourself, even if you weren't caught and punished.'

Stealing concerns girls strongly, too. 'Ashamed', 'guilty', 'sorry', 'unhappy' are the terms used, with the comment: 'You'd know you'd done wrong.' But the drowning situation evokes two responses, holding that if the girl did not help she would feel 'dreadful' and 'guilty'. Lying, too, even if undetected, 'starts bothering you after a while'; 'It's on your mind'; 'You'd know yourself.'

Thus fear merges into guilt feelings at 9 years. Higher intelligence, we observe, is associated with such guilt responses.

3 At 11 Years

Stealing still produces strong responses from boys. Heteronomous fear is expressed by 'afraid' and 'ashamed' – especially when linked with fear of Borstal and the comment, 'I'd tremble.' 'Guilty' and 'on his mind' are now familiar.

The term 'conscience' now appears. 'It comes from Satan'; 'It comes from Heaven'; 'You're born with it'; 'It keeps playing on your mind. It makes you own up in the end.'

With girls, too, the phrase 'on her mind' is clearly an expansion of 'guilty'. If unpunished, 'you'd still know it yourself'. Guilt is 'something that feels as if it's pressing on you all the time', and 'You'd feel you must tell somebody.'

Girls typically give more fulsome definitions of conscience. It is essentially 'an inside feeling', from God or the Devil, and 'you are born with it'. But girls expressively personify conscience: 'It's a little man inside you, prodding you all the time'; 'It's like a person nagging inside, and we know we've done wrong even if no one else does.' A definitive response is: 'It's two little voices. One tells you to do right, the other tells you to do wrong. The good one is from God, the bad one from Satan. Our good conscience tells us when we've done wrong.'

4 At 13 Years

Climacteric development is yet again revealed at 13 years. The majority of children use the term 'conscience'; and it is now that we find it evoked more by the Value of Life Test than by the Stealing Test.

Conscience is variously located in boys' responses: 'It's a feeling from your heart'; 'It's in our mind'; 'It's a feeling that bothers you, in your brain'. Its source, too, is variously defined: 'It's put there by God from birth'; 'It's like Jesus talking to us'; 'It's like a little voice inside: you feel guilty, you make up the voice.' But the real source of conscience is now beginning to be recognised: 'Rules and laws tell us it's wrong, in the first place'; It's formed by your upbringing'; 'You're born with it: your parents and friends help it grow.'

For girls, too, the matter of life and death is now the most evocative situation. Responses now become familiar: 'It's in your heart. It grows; you feel more. You learn from parents.' And again: 'It's inside your brain. You're born with it. You learn from parents, teachers and friends.' A new aspect of the concept of conscience is that 'it grows through doing wrong'. It is activated by each act of wrongdoing and thereby developed; so that 'the more wrong you do, the more you get a bad conscience'. The need to unburden is typified in the response: 'I'd have to tell someone in the end.'

5 At 15 Years

Definitions are now so familiar as to need no repetition. The Value of Life Test is now outstanding in evoking conscience, whereas stealing and lying do not. Even if wrongdoing is unknown by others, 'you still feel guilty', 'you still worry'; in short, 'you punish yourself'. A terse masculine definition is: 'Every rotten thing you do sticks in your mind.'

From girls, too, we get a similar pattern. Conscience is still thought of as innate, but as developing. You 'keep thinking', 'worry', 'feel awful', 'can't forget it'. But a new understanding of conscience appears in the response: 'It's something you get as you grow up. If we had been brought up alone, without being with people, we wouldn't have a conscience.'

6 At 17 Years

Only one boy fails to cite conscience in one or other situation. Descriptive phrases are: 'It plays on your mind'; 'You can't sleep. You feel rotten;' 'It bugs you all the time'; 'It's always digging at you'; 'It preys on your mind. You punish yourself.' A definitive response is: 'It's a mental reaction. It plays on your mind and matures with it. It's a sense of right and wrong, developed by school, your upbringing, your parents. Religion would help it, if you were religious – it would make a strong conscience.'

As before, the term 'awful' is typically used by girls to describe guilt feelings. One suggests that it may change with mood. For another, it is 'a high sense of guilt which haunts you all the time'. The origin of conscience is now clearly seen: 'Conscience is given to you by others. You'd have no conscience without other people – except for killing. It changes as you grow.' And therefore: 'If you were brought up like Kim, you wouldn't have any feelings of guilty conscience.'

The Genesis of Conscience

We may now sum up the genesis of conscience as revealed by this developmental response pattern.

At 7 years there is no evidence of interiorised moral feelings. The issue of life and death brings out strong native sympathy, merging into a sense of reciprocity in 8% of the age-group. For the rest, the dominant atmosphere is of heteronomous fear of detection and of consequent punishment.

At 9 years such fear merges into inner discomfort, typically expressed as 'guilt', in 25% of the age-group. Such fear and guilt are, of course, found in later age-groups, though naturally decreasing. Thus, 23% of the 11-year age-group express guilt feelings not yet developed into conscience, a figure reduced to 8% at 13 years.

At 11 years the term 'conscience' first appears, being used by 38% of the age-group. Since a further 23% express guilt feelings, we observe interiorised moral feelings in 61% of this age-group. Conscience is personified, typically by girls, and a minority define it in probably religious terms – verbalisms.

At 13 years conscience responses are doubled, 73% using and, of course, defining the term. Guilt and conscience responses combined show 81% of this age-group to have interiorised moral emotions, an increase of 20%. Here too, then, in terms of conscience we see the familiar climacteric development. The term 'conscience' is now used in responses to more than one test, though frequency of use of the term is not evidence of a stronger concept. But conscience is more clearly defined: it is in the mind; it is a social construct; it is exercised and thereby strengthened by wrongdoing; relief comes only through unburdening. Religious references now become minimal: the 'voice of God' and the 'voice of Satan' now become 'the good half and the bad half of you'.

At 15 years, after so massive an advance, little more of significance can be expected. Indeed, as elsewhere, we find at 15 years a standing-still, if not a regression, in moral judgement. Thus, 68% cite conscience as compared with 73% at 13 years, while 12% express guilt-feelings as compared with 8% at 13 years. The situation involving life and death is now outstanding in evoking conscience. It is increasingly recognised as the moral capacity, potential from birth, but actualised by society, chiefly through parents and teachers.

At 17 years, 97% cite conscience, a massive increase of 29% over the 15-year age-group. The process of interiorisation is now complete. Religious references are rare. Conscience 'comes from society'; 'some people seem not to have one'; 'You'd have no conscience without other people.'

We must emphasise, however, that the 97% of conscience citations at 17 years by no means imply anything like perfect autonomy in this mature age-group. We recall that 45% of all conscience responses were derived from the issue of life and death, when to abandon the drowning person would be, as so many say, 'murder'; and that this was predominantly so in the older age-groups. Conscience may well be aroused by killing – the most heinous offence to every human society. But that by no means implies that conscience will be similarly aroused by, say, offences against property or offences that strike at the heart of human relationships. Conscience, we repeat, is limited both in quality and in quantity – in the strength of its command, in the area of its control.

With this vital caveat we can, nonetheless, perceive a broad development. It proceeds from the fear of heteronomy to the guilt of interiorised and universalised precepts, and culminates in the autonomy we know as conscience.

Autonomy in Action

We may fittingly conclude this account of autonomy with a concrete example of its working. No situation could be more revealing of its functioning than that of truth-telling. Cheating is too insignificant to children, and saving life too intense; stealing involves obvious, serious practical risks. But lying is no criminal offence; and, once heteronomy has lost its sway and the controls of social praise and blame are no longer dominant, the only control must be personal and interior. We can agree with Piaget that the realisation of lying as breaking trust reveals dawning autonomy; and it is interesting that we find this first solidly appearing at 13 years, with all the other hallmarks of autonomy.

1 Consistency

We analysed children's judgements on lying from a number of areas. One of them was concerned with lying on behalf of a friend. We asked three questions: Whether it would be legitimate to lie for a friend to help him, to save him from trouble, and by not telling on him.

But we first asked whether lying was always wrong, in order to seek evidence later for consistency. Heteronomy has at least the virtue of consistency; and 92% of 7-year children dutifully affirm that lying is always wrong. At 11 years the figure is still 77%. But, with the development that we have come to expect thereafter, insistence that lying is always wrong decreases; responses affirming this decrease to 62% at 13 years, 32% at 15 years and 18% at 17 years. Such results, far from implying anomy, are evidence of autonomy at work in a concrete situation.

2 White Lies

We can best analyse this evidence in terms of 'white' lies, grouping responses to all three questions. The actual term does not appear often; even at 15 and 17 years it appears in only twelve and eleven responses respectively. But, of course, we add to such responses all those conditional responses that begin with the repeated phrase 'it all depends' – one, incidentally, that Piaget never seemed to meet.

This appears in forty-six responses at 15 years and in eighty at 17 years. Thus, of responses to all three questions, 32% at 15 years and 50% at 17 years are conditional in holding that everything depends upon the situation.

But this is by no means to hold – as does the new school of 'situation ethics' – that the individual brings nothing to the situation save a broad, blanket principle of love. 'White' lies can only be defined in terms of 'black' lies – which, of course, they assume. And the phrase 'it all depends' similarly assumes the rule that lying is wrong in itself. Thus, we see the adaptation of the principle of truth-telling to the actual situation – that is, autonomy at work.

At 9 years we find the first evidences of such a process, if minimal. 'White lies might be all right', says one; 'not if it's little fibs that don't hurt', says another, introducing a basic principle. A boy gives a definition brilliant in both simplicity and clarity: 'It's right in my own way, but not in Teacher's way.'

At 11 years white lies are all right – for example, 'to small children who don't understand'. Boys typically suggest the legitimacy of lying by an escaping prisoner of war, in self-defence, and in fighting crime.

At 13 years a white lie begins to be defined. It is 'a bit of truth and a bit of lie'; such lies are 'very small ones that don't really hurt anyone'; they are 'like a story, not to mean any harm'. Specific instances are given, too: lying to conceal birthday presents; to keep a promise 'not to tell'; and, in chilly reciprocity, 'to pay back a lie told to you'. Lying is all right 'if you're defending a close friend or parent'; and so 'if someone you loved and trusted was in trouble'.

The development at 15 years is strong. The legitimacy of a doctor concealing the truth from his patient is instanced in a few responses. White lies are those which 'avoid hurting someone's feelings', which 'help someone else', which are 'for the good of someone else'. Loyalty is expressed by: 'I value his friendship more highly than Teacher's trust.'

Conditional responses increase to 50% at 17 years. A new sophistication is the typically feminine agreement to false compliments, as is the legitimacy of lying 'when the truth might break friendship'. White lies are to 'protect people from harmful truth'; 'to help someone else'; 'to save hurting a person's feelings'. In short, 'hurting people is more serious than telling white lies'; and the ultimate definition: 'Lying is all right for reasons of love.'

3 Conditionality

In this developing pattern we see the application of a known and interiorised principle – that lying is wrong – to concrete situations. It gives no support for Piaget's theory that autonomy, in this situation above all, is born of reciprocity; nor for the situation ethics that hold judgement to be intuited from the situation. Lying is wrong – that is the basic premise, born, undoubtedly, of heteronomy. But the principle must be applied and adapted to the situation.

Judgement, therefore, 'depends' – on motives, relationships, circumstances, obligations. While lying is wrong, it is permissible under certain clearly defined conditions – that no one else is hurt; that the trouble must not be serious, nor deserving of severe punishment; that there is a real personal relationship of loyalty, friendship or love. Thus, far from breaking personal relationships, such lying is expressly permitted, since it is required by them. Conversely, the principle of truth-telling may not be overridden for the benefit of self; nor to save another from the just deserts of serious wrongdoing, a bad lie being, in broad definition, a big lie; nor if, in helping one, another is thereby hurt. The whole concern throughout is for the well-being of the other person; lying for selfish reasons is *ipso facto* wrong.

Here, then, is autonomy in action. None of our subjects, from 9 years upwards, judged lying to be right in principle. Few show the selfish indifference of: 'I wouldn't like to get involved.' Few, too, are so concreted in a rigid rule of truth-telling as to hold even white lies to be wrong. The situations concerned involved free relationships with peers *vis-à-vis* authority. The dilemma involved is of adhering *both* to the principle of truth-telling *and* to the obligations of loyalty, friendship or love. Some – typically girls – comfort themselves with the subtle casuistry of 'saying nothing is not telling lies'. Many, as they mature, put the person above the principle.

4 Autonomy in Maturity

Such subordination of rules to persons might be interpreted as a weakening of autonomy. On the contrary, it is a profoundly Christian insight. 'Truth-telling was made for man, not man for truth-telling.' It is typical evidence of the rational-altruistic conscience at work.

But here, too, it would be quite wrong to assume that maturing young people, or even a majority of them, share such a rational-altruistic autonomy. Only 50% of all responses to all three questions show such enlightened moral judgement, if deriving in the main from the 15- and 17-year age-groups. But at 17 years we still find 18% of responses strictly insisting that lying is always wrong in all circumstances; and even 15% who still approve of telling tales. Such rigidity of judgement is the expression of either continuing heteronomy or of rigid reciprocity. Even in the intimate relationship with parents, to illustrate from another area, we find 15% of responses at 17 years dominated by heteronomy, and a further 23% which legalistically insist that lying is always wrong to parents. Neither group can conceive any circumstances in which love might make stronger demands than rules.

Other factors are, of course, involved here – not least the nature of the authority imposed by heteronomy, and the nature of the individual. Heteronomy must have its place if autonomy is ever to be achieved. But only heteronomy inspired and guided by love can breed that rational and altruistic autonomy which subordinates rules to persons and moral principles to the overriding claims of love.

Part Two
Factors in Development

6
Intelligence

Factors Involved

Reasoning must play a part in moral development, as in every other part of the child's growth. A learning process and the acquisition of essential knowledge are involved here, as everywhere. Moral skill has to be learnt like any other. The imbecile, or the feral child who has never developed human powers of reasoning, cannot acquire moral skill. But, on the other hand, the complete psychopath – the moral imbecile – may not be lacking in power to reason. Thus the place of intelligence is by no means clear-cut.

1 The Nature of Intelligence

Studies of intelligence show it to be much more complex than traditional intelligence tests have assumed. In particular, verbal reasoning tests obviously involve verbal facility, so that the child from a less favourable cultural background is at a disadvantage. By contrast, the child with parents who have devoted time to reasoning and discussing moral questions develops, not only verbal skills, but also clearer concepts. Raw heteronomy will punish the child for an offence, and there the matter ends. But when the nature of the offence has been discussed and reasoned, moral skill has been developed.

Piaget, for his part, was concerned with pure cognition. He held two factors only to be involved in the development of moral judgement – co-operation and intelligence. 'Co-operation, of course, presupposes intelligence, but this circular relation is perfectly natural: intelligence animates co-operation and yet needs this social instrument for its own formation' (Piaget, op.cit., 168). A number of questions are begged here. The nature of intelligence is never defined. It is assumed that it alone promotes the sociality of co-operation.

Moreover, we find the familiar theory that mutual co-operation between peers is the sole instrument by which moral judgement is developed.

But concepts are seldom purely cognitive. Orectic, non-cognitive factors are involved. Moral concepts, as we have seen, have their emotional loading – whether of fear, or guilt, or the developed conscience. Above all, the motivation for moral behaviour is at least as important as moral knowledge. Piaget typically concerned himself with 'moral judgement'; and his typical approach – 'What *should* he do?' is of a piece with this concern. But to think of intelligence as a cool, objective judge, calmly weighing the evidence, is grossly inadequate. All our evidence is of moral concepts, heavily weighted with emotion, that express inner attitudes – not judicial decisions. The very phrase 'moral judgement' is too slender to carry such a load; and any approach that seeks to ignore subjective, emotional, orectic aspects of moral decision must fail to do justice to the total human personality in its moral behaviour.

There is a cognitive aspect of moral judgement; and some studies may be so framed as to evoke cognitive judgements rather than emotionally-toned attitudes. Their value may be questioned. Piaget himself goes so far, at one point, as to find it 'conceivable that intelligence alone might suffice to sharpen the child's evaluation of conduct without necessarily inclining him to do good actions' (Piaget, op.cit., III f.). It is the inner self-criticism of guilt that is the most powerful moral control, not the cold light of reason.

2 *Development in Intelligence*

We have constantly observed the climacteric stage of development to fall between 11 and 13 years – that is, with the onset of adolescence. This, too, corresponds with Piaget's onset of the highest stage in intellectual development of 'formal operations', when the mind achieves the ability to think in abstractions. Thus specific moral concepts, built up over the years through experience, can now develop into general concepts of moral qualities and ideals. We might thus superficially assume that development in intelligence is the primary factor in this dramatic growth.

Such a conclusion might appear to be supported by our finding that the greatest disparity in intelligence between boys and girls is at 11 and 13 years. Thus, earlier development in girls would account for their higher intelligence: and higher intelligence for their higher moral insights. Since the children of 11 years were from the same classes, schools, estates and, possibly in some cases, even homes, such a sex difference in intelligence could not be accounted for by selectivity.

The hormones poured into the bloodstream at the onset of puberty must affect the whole person, and thus by no means simply develop secondary sexual characteristics. Development in mind and in personality must also follow; and, with them, changes in social and moral attitudes. Adolescence, therefore, is not only a matter of physical and intellectual development. With it comes the growth of ideals, as illustrated by conversion experiences and search for a master sentiment. Intelligence, therefore, is not the sole factor to be considered in moral development.

In the various moral areas with which we have been concerned, we find ample evidence of other factors at work besides intelligence. We may instance the greater sympathy of girls at 7 years; their markedly superior development of insight into the nature of lying at 9 years, when the mean intelligence of boys exceeds theirs; their greater sensitivity to personal relationships throughout, and in particular at 17 years, when we can assume that development as such is completed. The cheating situation was deliberately used to explore the place of intelligence; for here, above all, intelligence alone might well achieve the realisation that cheating is sheer folly: 'You only cheat yourself.' Certainly intelligence showed itself strongly associated with moral judgements on cheating – but slightly less so, in fact, than in judgements on lying. It was by no means the only factor involved, even conscience being cited. Nor was the pattern of response consistent in its relationship with intelligence. Nor, again, did comparison with results from other situations support such a relationship.

Statistical analysis certainly showed intelligence to be the most noteworthy of the variable factors in its positive association with moral judgements; and outstandingly so in the responses of girls. Their judgements at 11 years showed an almost total pattern of association with intelligence; but an almost complete lack of association at 13 years, when their advantage, in terms of mean intelligence, is scarcely less strong. A strong, positive pattern was again evident in girls of 15 years – when, however, their supposed advantage of higher mean intelligence was greatly reduced.

In short, we find other factors, in addition to intelligence, to be at work in children's responses to projection tests. The judgements elicited were seldom objective and detached judicial decisions, as quotations have shown. In particular, the sex difference cannot be wholly ascribed to earlier development of intelligence in girls at 11 and 13 years. Boys show marked development at 13 years in their judgements upon saving life, cheating and stealing – and this despite the supposed handicap of markedly lower mean intelligence. That they showed no such development in the lying situation until 15 years is simply the measure of the far greater feminine sensitivity to personal relationships.

The Place of Intelligence

While, therefore, we cannot give intelligence the sole place in moral judgement, we can see that it is essential. Its functions are manifest.

1 Reciprocity

We can agree with Piaget in seeing reason at work in the development of a sense of reciprocity – without, however, agreeing that it is the source of autonomy. Reasoning sees the logic of A treating B as B treats A.

But more than intelligence is involved. Most of our evidence for reciprocity came from the drowning situation; and we observed it to develop from natural sympathy. Piaget agrees in seeing that the play of sympathy gives rise to a sense of reciprocity.

Moreover, far from maturing inexorably and universally into autonomy, we found reciprocity to remain as a level of moral judgement for some in maturity. As such, its characteristics appear as a strict *quid pro quo* in relationships with others, and a concern for self that leaves small room for disinterested altruism. Such calculated reciprocity may well indicate a primarily cognitive approach to others. It has no seeds within itself of higher judgement. If B does not respond in like manner strict reciprocity does not of itself counsel understanding and forgiveness. It is of the head, rather than of the heart. It lacks the milk of human kindness.

2 Foreseeing Consequences

Intelligence clearly has a place in foreseeing the consequences of actions; and this is one of the ground-rules for all moral behaviour. Acting with a due regard for the consequences of one's actions involves the ability to foresee them. To act otherwise is to act purely on impulse, and such is the behaviour of the psychopath.

But it is questionable whether a very high level of intelligence is required to conceive the likely results of a course of action. Limited intelligence may have a harder job of it, particularly in more involved situations. But experience – above all, of rewards and punishments, both natural and human – is a great teacher. The resulting habits deal with the majority of everyday situations, and so do away with the necessity for intense and constant reasoning.

Any moral code must be reasonable – and, so far as possible, seen to be reasonable. The truly moral man has a rational autonomy, and makes his own decisions on the basis of reason together with altruistic concern for others. One of the essential characteristics of true heteronomy is to help children to weigh the likely consequences of their actions, and to give experience of doing this, together with the encouragement and discouragement of rewards and punishments.

But more than reason is involved. Feeling for others, both sympathy and empathy, is essential. Above all, imagination has a great part to play in foreseeing the consequences of actions – as, indeed, in all moral judgement. And imagination itself can powerfully support reason in the process.

3 Judging Consequences

Reason is involved, not only in foreseeing the likely results of actions, but also in passing judgement upon them; and thereby, through experience, building up a rational morality.

But here, too, both head and heart are involved. Judgement itself must be made in the light of some yardstick, whether it be advantage to self, benevolence to others, or the good of the community. But it is the emotional tone of such self-criticism that is all-important to the individual. Feelings of guilt are at the heart of autonomy, as are feelings of self-respect after actions that have not offended the moral self. Hence the deep truth enshrined in Ernest Hemingway's simple definition: 'What's good is what I feel good after. What's bad is what I feel bad after.'

4 Foreseeing Remote Goals

Intelligence functions, too, in being able to conceive remote goals. As such it can conceive the value of foregoing immediate and legitimate satisfaction for the sake of a far greater, though far more distant, satisfaction. The immediate interest of the adolescent, for example, is to leave school and to start earning money, with all that it brings – not least, independence. Intelligence cannot only see the likely minimal prospects in such employment. It can also foresee the distant but ultimately far greater satisfaction of acquiring a profession, though the cost be years of dedicated study. The younger, the less able the individual, the greater will be the appeal of immediate satisfaction.

But here, too, other factors are involved. A boy's identification with a professional father may be a strong factor in continuing with study. Similarly, a working man's determination that his son should achieve a skilled career may be a powerful incentive. Strong motivation is involved if the distant goal is to be patiently pursued; and, again, imagination can be a powerful support to achieve what reason dictates.

5 *Moral Learning*

Moral skill has to be learnt, so that intelligence is involved in learning the rules imposed by heteronomy and in understanding both their meaning and application. The nature of the heteronomy used is, of course, crucial. The more able child can more easily perceive the relevance and reasonableness of rules, assuming that they are reasonable. The less able child needs more patient teaching and longer experience. Authoritarianism can stultify both.

But here, as in every aspect of morality, intelligence does not work in a vacuum. We have seen suggestion and identification to be strong roots of the moral self, even without specific moral teaching. To understand rules is not necessarily to practise them. Motivation is all-important.

6 *Resolving Conflicts*

We have seen one of the limitations of conscience, as the normal guide to conduct, to arise when it is divided. The very question, 'What shall I do?' is the clearest evidence that conscience has given no answer. To be more precise, autonomy is the application of accepted and interiorised ideals to moral situations. But, since situations differ, and no two are ever exactly alike, moral judgement consists in the adaptation of the ideals to each situation. It is not a matter of applying one single ideal. Such rigidity can be both irrational and inhuman. It is a matter of grouping and regrouping accepted ideals to the circumstances.

Conflict lies at the heart of the moral life – not only between the natural and the moral self, but between the demands of moral attitude and the demands of the situation. Intelligence clearly plays a part here. We have seen this conflict strongly exposed in responses to the lying situation. The ideal of truth-telling conflicted with the claims of loyalty, of friendship, and of love. Some adhere rigidly to rules; others put persons above rules. The recognition of white lies resolves the conflict for many, as intelligence seeks to arbitrate between the opposing claims.

Such conflicts may be intense and long-lasting. If we use again the example of an adolescent continuing his education, aiming at a professional qualification, conflict may arise between his personal goal and loyalty to his parents, upon whom he may be imposing a heavy financial burden. Only careful reasoning of the arguments on both sides of the dilemma can bring a rational decision. But it is acted upon within the context of moral obligations and loyalties that involve far more than the cold light of reason.

Other Aspects of Intelligence

Such are the basic functions of intelligence in moral judgement. There are, however, other aspects of its functioning that suggest another side of the picture.

1 Gaining Approval

Intelligence is of great help in enabling the individual to conceive the kind of behaviour that will win the approval and avoid the condemnation of others. We have already seen, on the unconscious level, a similar process at work in the young child. Negatively, in terms of the super-ego, he must repress the aggressive impulses that threaten the love that is his deepest need. Positively, in terms of the ego-ideal, he builds up a picture of what he must be to win love.

On the conscious level, growing intelligence sees the conduct that will bring esteem and avoid censure. It is, therefore, of great assistance in enabling the intelligent child to conform to the demands of heteronomy. Wanting approval, he understands better how to win it. The less intelligent child, lacking such an understanding, has to plod on, step by step, learning one thing at a time.

But the advantage that intelligence gives in this respect in winning social approval has its own moral temptations. Conformity may be of the head, rather than of the heart – a matter of artificial calculation rather than of genuine attitude. The more able child can more easily calculate acceptable behaviour, and act accordingly. Such ability may well assist development in moral judgement. But it may, alternatively, promote hypocrisy.

2 Behaving Uprightly

Intelligence is also a direct asset in behaving uprightly. The less able child, competing with his peers, has temptations that simply do not arise for the more able. In our cheating situation, for example, it is the less able child who is tempted to cheat, and so needs the strong hand of heteronomy. It is the abler child who can progressively affirm that 'You don't learn by cheating', that 'It isn't fair on the others', that 'You're not being honest with yourself', that 'You're not showing what you can do', and, ultimately, 'I prefer to see my own results.' In short, 'You get more satisfaction doing it yourself,' says the abler child.

There are clearly many such situations in which intelligence is a powerful aid to upright behaviour, doing away with any need to descend to immoral expedients. A competitive system naturally increases temptations for the less able, whereas co-operation mini-mises them. Just as the child from an affluent home, well supplied with money, has less temptation to steal, so the abler child, well endowed with intelligence, has less temptation to cheat.

Yet such upright behaviour may bear little relation to moral attitudes, and have small moral content. It is not unknown for intelligence to overreach itself, having its own temptation of pride. The abler child may become the more adept at lying, for example, to gain his ends.

3 Plausibility

Hence a third asset that intelligence gives, of which lying is a good example. It is clear, on the one hand, that more able children are quicker to see the folly of lying, not least because it only leads to more trouble in the end; while the less able may proceed from lie to lie, getting themselves deeper in the mire. But, on the other hand, intelligence is more facile and agile, not only in more ingenious lying, but also in explaining away apparent offences. Such plausibility also lacks moral content.

Moreover, lying may become the supreme social tool of the very able child. With skilful lying he may become adept at manipulating people for his own ends, and so develop a lifelong habit. Hence the plausible rogues figuring in crime reports who are by no means lacking in intelligence. Such a child may become morally 'at risk', both in himself and to society, should his emotional environment be inadequate. Here again we see the weakness of Piaget's theory that intelligence plus social co-operation produce autonomy in truth-telling.

They may, in fact, produce an anomy the more dangerous to all concerned precisely because it has high intelligence at its command.

Emotion and Cognition in Moral Judgement

Some studies have distinguished between the cognitive and the emotional aspects of moral judgement. Some have, by their very approach, elicited the one more than the other.

It is patently clear that both are involved. On the one hand, we find evidence in all areas that higher moral judgements are associated with higher intelligence. Morality must be reasoned if it is to be anything more than the heteronomous obedience of the slave, or the social conformity dependent upon social praise and blame – both external to the self. It must, therefore, have a solid cognitive nucleus. Lacking it, neither the imbecile nor the non-human feral child can make moral judgements. Possessing it, the able child has all the potential advantages that we have seen higher intelligence to bestow.

But the complex responses of children to moral situations of key significance to them rarely ever show pure cognition by itself. There is always some emotional content to the moral concepts they express. Lacking moral feelings, the amoral and the psychopathic have no moral controls. It is in feelings of fear and of guilt – not in cognitive understanding – that we see the genesis of the moral self.

But, just as a fierce super-ego can be pathological in irrational control, so can intelligence be cunning in unfeelinged pursuit of its end. If the moral self can be irrational, intelligence can be immoral. Both emotion and cognition are involved in moral living with others. The highest relationship between persons known to man is love. But

such love is neither wholly a matter of cold reason, nor wholly a
matter of emotion, even less of sentimentality. It is an attitude of
goodwill, volitional in its expression of the whole person, rather than
solely emotional or solely cognitive. Moral concepts involve both
reason and emotion.

The Place of Non-moral Knowledge

Just as religious thinking is the application of the normal processes
of reasoning to religion, so does moral thinking involve a similar
application of the mind to moral concerns. Such moral thinking is
clearly a vital factor, though not the only factor, involved in moral
judgement; and through such judgements, made in concrete situations, moral skills are developed, and a body of moral knowledge is
built up.

But no less necessary to moral judgement is knowledge that is not of
itself, moral. A basic principle of all morality is to act with a due
regard for the consequences of actions. This principle is not basic in
the sense that it may promote higher moral conduct. It could, of
itself, lead to no more than a morality of expediency that rises little
above the concern with resulting pain and pleasure that controls
anomy. But it is a basic principle in that it must enter into every
moral judgement, whatever its level. Now it presupposes knowledge
of the relationship between cause and effect. It requires an understanding of actions as having consequences, that is, in the moral
sphere. Such knowledge of causal connections applies, of course, to
many aspects of life; and, therefore, to other aspects of education. It
is, therefore, non-moral. It thus clearly illustrates the necessity of
non-moral knowledge to moral judgement.

Another example is that of motivation. As we have seen, moral
judgement is not merely the simple application of moral knowledge to
the situation. The individual by no means always acts upon what he
knows to be right. What is lacking in such a situation is the motivation. But again, morality involves not simply having effective motives
to activate conduct. It also involves knowing what those motives are.
Now perception of one's motives is not by any means limited to
strictly moral concerns. It, too, relates to many other aspects of life;
and, therefore, to other aspects of education. It is certainly true that
in the moral sphere apparently altruistic behaviour may, in fact, be
motivated by covert self-interest – that, like Becket in T. S. Eliot's

Murder in the Cathedral, the individual may be consciously tempted 'to do the right thing for the wrong reason', or may unconsciously act thus. Perception of one's true motives is essential to genuine morality. But such perception is not, of itself, strictly moral knowledge.

Moral Judgement

If we may now seek a broad definition of moral judgement, we can say at once that it is by no means unitary. Clearly, it has a number of constituent parts.

Native intelligence has a key place, not only in making a moral analysis of the concrete situation, but also in bringing to bear upon it such non-moral knowledge as has been acquired in other life experiences and in other areas of education.

But reason alone is not enough; of itself it may conceive and practise the subtlest immorality. Moral judgement also involves, secondly, those orectic factors, and not least the emotional, which we find to heavily tone the moral concepts of children, and so to colour their moral judgements.

Hence, thirdly, the motivating drives, conscious or unconscious, that activate moral behaviour and direct it towards its goal. Without the dynamics of motivation, the known good may well remain undone.

Nor can we omit, finally, the native sympathy that is the root of all social living, and the power of native imagination to reinforce the dictates of reason.

Moral judgement thus becomes a shorthand term for the various aspects of the total personality expressed in its encounter with other persons. To conceive of it as no more than cognitive activity is to misconceive it.

7
Sex Differences

Problems of Testing

Studies of moral judgement have not revealed a clear-cut distinction between the sexes. There have been some indications that girls develop conscience earlier than boys, but trends have been found, rather than conclusive evidence.

Piaget notes in his work that 'all the subjects are boys unless the letter G is added', because 'the legal sense is far less developed in little girls than in boys' (Piaget, op.cit., 27, 69). A study thus broadly limited to one sex may be justified, given an essentially cognitive approach; but, of course, it ignores possible sex differences in intelligence itself, as well as in attitudes. Studies following upon Piaget's work have also tended to use boys only.

Only once does Piaget observe a sex difference, and that is in the context of physical aggression. Boys, he finds, tend to repay more, and girls to repay less, than the blows received. But a type of situation involving physical aggression – also used in other studies – would seem quite inadequate to define sex differences in moral judgement; it might well illustrate no more than the different sex roles in society. Such differences can only be effectively observed by testing over a wide area of moral situations known to be of outstanding significance to both sexes, and by using an equal number of boys and girls at each age-level. In this kind of testing, we found girls to be in advance of boys in their moral judgements in every area examined.

Two points, however, must be made. First, if we assume a close relationship between intelligence and moral judgement, the earlier development of girls would give them an advantage – and so reduce the significance of their higher judgements. This point has already been discussed; and we shall observe further relevant factors in this chapter. Secondly, the stronger native ability of girls in verbalising may not only facilitate the development of intelligence, and so of moral concepts. It may also produce more expansive and subtle responses, such as to make them appear more developed in their judgements as compared with boys lacking their flow of speech. Girls were, on the whole, more fluent than boys – though less so in the higher range of intelligence. But the situations used were significant and evocative to both sexes; each was examined in depth, as well as in its various aspects; and where one approach reached a dead end another was adopted.

In practice, boys were as keen as girls to give their judgements. In the event, sex differences were thereby exposed in both verbal and written tests.

Differences in Verbal Tests

1 Levels of Judgement – All Four Tests

In responses revealing anomy, boys have the melancholy distinction of leading girls at every age after 7 years, when the sexes are broadly similar. In girls' responses, anomy is minimal after 11 years. In boys' responses it is some 10% at both 13 and 15 years, and still 5% at 17 years.

Boys, too, are distinguished by their greater reliance upon, and therefore need of, heteronomy. Only at 9 years do girls' responses show greater heteronomy; and this, we suggested, may indicate their stronger universalising of heteronomous rules. From the age of 13 years, the turning-point in development, boys show much more heteronomy; and still at 17 years their 17% compares with the 7% in girls' responses.

In the area of socionomy, we observe in girls a stronger sympathy leading to somewhat stronger reciprocity, and a keener awareness of social relationships, in the earlier age-groups. But it is at 15 and again at 17 years that there is a massive difference between the sexes. Girls show a far greater insight into personal relationships and therefore a far greater sensitivity to them. Even this, however, does not mean that the boys lead, at these ages, in the higher level of autonomy; for in autonomy the sexes are broadly similar. The immense lead of the girls in socionomy at 15 and 17 years is, in fact, due to so many boys' responses being rooted in the lower levels of anomy and heteronomy.

Autonomy first dawns at 11 years, with girls already showing much stronger signs of it than boys. But so enormous is the advance of the girls at 13 years – from 19% to 45% of responses indicating autonomy – that they show small development thereafter. The parallel development in boys does not appear until 15 years, an age-group later. Further development in boys at 17 years brings the sexes broadly together in their total autonomy.

The overall picture, therefore, from responses to all four situations is one of boys leading girls strongly in the two lowest levels of moral judgement, anomy and heteronomy; and they lead throughout, as well as in the mature age-group of 17 years. Girls lead boys in socionomy throughout, and most strongly so in maturity. Girls make a far earlier and stronger development to autonomy than do boys.

2 Saving Life

Given the profound relevance of the situation to moral judgement, we can also observe sex differences in response to different types of situation. Each, naturally, will bring out its own type of response, and therefore each will throw light on sex differences from a new viewpoint.

In the stark issue of life and death, we observe at 7 years the much stronger innate sympathy of girls, developing into a sense of reciprocity. While at 9 and 11 years, the classic period of reciprocity, such responses are strong in both sexes, girls still lead boys. Similarly, with the classic development of autonomy manifest at 13 years, while both sexes show marked development, girls show it more strongly than boys. Boys catch up with girls at 15 years – again, an age-group later – and the sexes are similar in their autonomy in the two oldest age-groups.

Thus, even in the most vital moral situation of all, we see girls in advance of boys in sympathy, in reciprocity, and in the development of autonomy. We might, of course, say that especially in such a situation is a marked sex difference to be expected if, with McDougall, we hold the maternal instinct to be the matrix of all altruism; or if, with Piaget, we hold compassion to be an 'instinctive tendency' and such sympathy to fire reason to become aware of reciprocity.

Conversely, boys lead girls throughout in their responses even to this situation in their anomy and heteronomy. Lacking such strong innate sympathy, these two lowest levels are most marked in boys at 7 years. Thereafter they naturally fade; but, whereas they disappear from girls' responses at 13 years, they are still 12% in boys' responses at 15 years, and do not become minimal until 17 years.

3 Cheating

In the cheating situation, by contrast, intelligence is a more significant factor, though by no means the only one. Girls show their first overall development at 11 years, and again, with typical strength, at 13 years – so much so that not until 17 years do boys reach the development achieved by girls at 13 years. Girls therefore lead boys in the three maturing age-groups by a similar figure, so that intelligence is not the key factor.

Boys, again, lead girls in anomy and heteronomy throughout, save for girls' greater heteronomy at 9 years, and again at 17 years. Striking, too, is the development of girls in socionomy at 15 and 17 years, with but a slight lead in autonomy at these maturing ages. But again we find girls developing in autonomy an age-group ahead of boys.

4 Stealing

While the temptation of stealing is predominantly a male problem, the overall response pattern is familiar. Boys lead throughout in both anomy and heteronomy, if less strongly. Girls again show a pronounced development in socionomy at 15 and 17 years. Girls develop in autonomy at 11 and 13 years; boys do not show their strong development until 15 years, again an age-group later.

In the subordinate situation of finding money, girls show development at 11 years, and so strong an advance at 13 years that thereafter they remain static. Even socionomy pales before this intense, interiorised sense of honesty in girls that is developed at 13 years.

5 Lying

It is the lying situation, piercing to the heart of personal relationships, that reveals a unique pattern and the strongest sex difference.

Girls here make their first solid advance as early as 9 years. Reciprocity, hurting others, getting others into trouble, social blame, a sense of guilt – all these are factors in this uniquely early development in girls. Boys, by contrast, show uniquely late development, remaining static until 15 years, when they make their first movement, followed by another at 17 years.

In terms of autonomy, girls have completed their development at 13 years with a measure of autonomy not reached by boys until 17 years. But girls continue to develop in socionomy from 13 years upwards.

6 The Emerging Pattern

From these four test situations we observe a broadly similar pattern emerging. The climacteric stage of development is broadly between 11 and 13 years for both sexes. But there is immense difference between the sexes, not least in terms of quality. Girls are early developers in moral judgement; boys are late developers. While girls, with their innate advantages, leap ahead in insights and attitudes, boys progress slowly and far less spectacularly. Above all, we see the distinction in terms of autonomy. Whereas, at 13 years, boys are broadly emerging from heteronomy, girls of that age generally achieve so great a depth of autonomy that there is small progress thereafter. It is not, therefore, until 17 years that the sexes come within reach of each other in moral judgement; and even then girls still remain in advance of boys.

In the basic issue of life and death there is not to be expected an outstanding sex difference, save that girls show greater initial sympathy, and greater depth of autonomy at 13 years. But in terms of personal relationships boys are way behind girls in their moral insight, as seen in terms of lying. It is interesting, here, to recall that Piaget tested boys because of their stronger legalistic sense, and saw the first signs of autonomy in the realisation that lying breaks trust. It is in this very situation that we observe the most outstanding revelation of the higher moral judgements of girls – bearing in mind that the whole concern of morality is with relationships between persons.

Girls have the innate advantages of greater sympathy, stronger feeling for others, and therefore more profound sensitivity to personal relationships and social attitudes. They therefore develop earlier than boys in their moral judgements. Boys, progressing later and more slowly, finally reach a level of autonomy at 17 years that approximates to that of girls. But this does not mean that the sexes are broadly equal in maturity. At 17 years boys still show a solid measure of both anomy and heteronomy; girls have so developed as to replace these lower levels with their far stronger socionomy. Whatever place intelligence may be allotted in the earlier development of girls, the final picture is of a higher level of moral judgement in girls such as has been observable throughout.

Differences in Written Tests

1 Virtues and Vices

Such a sex difference in moral judgement is revealed no less strongly in written tests, used in addition to the verbal tests to seek ancillary evidence. We may illustrate from three areas.

One written test asked children to list what they regarded as the outstanding vices and virtues. For personal and altruistic virtues combined, girls provided 55% of responses and boys the remaining 45%. The sex difference is even more pronounced in terms of personal vices. Here girls provide 64% of responses and boys 36%. Boys are in their element when it comes to the physical, as contrasted with the psychological, aspects of personal relationships. Thus, the sex difference is at its lowest in terms of offences against the person.

In offences against property boys really come into their own, providing 58% of responses as compared with the girls' 42%. They also contribute 61% of responses concerned with cruelty to animals; whereas conversely, in recognising the positive virtue of kindness to animals, girls provide 57% of responses. Self-indulgence, too, is overwhelmingly a male concern, with 77% of responses.

Girls, in short, are skilled in the niceties, both good and bad, of interpersonal relationships; boys excel in the concrete situation. Girls are mainly concerned with the personal, boys with the physical; girls with being, boys with doing. Girls deplore such failings as meanness, cattiness, and jealousy, of which boys are scarcely aware; their citations of personal vices are almost double those of boys. Such differences are patent from 11 years, when development begins, and similar at all ages thereafter. Thus, at 17 years, girls are far more concerned than boys with lying, deceit, unkindness, and selfishness.

2 Conflict of Virtues and Vices

A further test sought evidence for children's judgements on the moral conflict between virtue and vice: and also upon the far more intense conflict between virtue and virtue – when, that is, a real dilemma is involved in a conflict of values. Four stories, consisting of everyday moral situations, were used under each of the two categories.

In the category of vice in conflict with virtue, girls led boys throughout at every age. Their early development was strikingly manifested at 11 years, boys making their advance at 13 years. While the gap between the sexes was narrowed at 17 years, girls were still in advance of boys. The stronger social sense and sensitivity of girls were yet again apparent. The situational element in moral judgement naturally patterned the sex difference in the varying situations. It was of interest, too, to find boys more consistent than girls in response to all four situations. Such consistency, notoriously not a feminine trait, tended to involve a rigidity of judgement, and a subordination of persons to rules that feminine sensitivity to personal relationships cannot stomach.

In the category of virtue in conflict with virtue, a similar pattern emerges. Girls lead boys throughout in their higher judgements. From sex parity at 9 years, girls show their first advance at 11 years, while boys show the familiar climacteric at 13 years. And, while boys remain static thereafter, girls make advances at 13 years and again at 17 years such as to make the strongest sex difference in maturity. It appears, therefore, that in this subtler conflict between virtue and virtue, girls have far more insight than boys. The influence of the situation upon judgements was apparent in, for example, the girls' stronger concern for private health and public safety, their greater affection for animals, their intense sense of honesty, and an innate sympathy that can even prevent them achieving higher moral judgement.

It is interesting to observe that, in this more subtle area of the conflict of virtues, girls show greater consistency in their judgements to all four situations, and chiefly at the key ages of 13 and 17 years. Keener and subtler feminine insight is more able to judge between conflicting virtues, whereas the stolid male is more at home in the simpler judgement between black and white. The subtler the situation, the more does the female come into her own. And that this should be most striking at 17 years, when the difference in mean intelligence between boys and girls is minimal, is further evidence that moral judgement involves far more than intelligence.

3 Justice Concepts

A further test was concerned with children's ideas of justice, using Piaget-type situations. Piaget saw three stages of development in children's ideas of justice. The first, dominated by heteronomy, requires punishment; the second, dominated by reciprocity, requires strict equality; the third sees the development of an equity that takes circumstances, motives and relationships into account.

One story concerned physical aggression. Here, familiarly, girls lead boys throughout in higher moral judgements, most strongly at 11 years, with their earlier development, and again at 17 years. Boys make their only significant advance at 13 years, and thereafter decline somewhat to a static mean. Feminine aversion to physical violence, as we suggested earlier, must be involved in such a situation, as must the male predilection for it. Yet the fact remains that judgements upon this situation produce a pattern that is consistent with that derived from many other areas; and, in particular, confirms the familiar sex difference.

Another situation concerned pupils lending personal property to each other in the classroom. Responses were analysed in terms of heteronomy, reciprocity and equity. Since, in free relationships between peers, heteronomy disappears after 9 years, the broad distinction is between reciprocity and equity. Girls show a massive advance in equity at 13 years and boys at 15 years – yet again an age-group later. At 17 years, girls' responses show 50% equity as compared with the 24% of the boys.

Girls, in this situation, were held fast in strict reciprocity at both 9 and 11 years. Their responses dominated by reciprocity, a unique 100% at 11 years, have decreased to 50% at 17 years, whereas 76% of boys' responses at 17 years still insist upon reciprocity. So much for the Piagetian theory that the free play of reciprocity between peers tends of itself towards autonomy.

The 15-year Age-group

We have been concerned, in this chapter, to portray from various areas the pattern of developing moral judgement, thereby elucidating the sex difference. One subordinate detail in this pattern deserves notice.

At 15 years, in many areas, we observe a standing still, in development; and, in some cases, an actual, if small, regression. This is true of both verbal and written tests. As we have so often observed, there are dramatic developments at 11 and 13 years; and, in many cases, a further advance at 17 years. But the difference in the 15-year age-group is not simply a matter of stability between developmental surges. It appears, rather, as if children at this age are often poised between further advance and decline – as if there is such uncertainty that development may be either to saint or to sinner.

This wavering at 15 years appears in both boys and girls, though it is of course, true that we have found, in some areas, a development of socionomy in girls at this age. It will, moreover, be characteristic of less autonomous individuals. Those dependent upon external sanctions could clearly go in either direction, forwards or backwards. Such a finding, in terms of moral development, strongly suggests the need for wise guidance at this age; and leaving school to plunge into a welter of conflicting moral codes may be by no means the best expedient.

Once this stage is over, however, we generally find further development at 17 years – boys making up some of the ground lost in their rather pedestrian progress, and girls developing not so much in autonomy – a process often complete for them at 13 years – as in their awareness of and response to personal relationships and to social living.

The sex difference is, however, manifest throughout, and in all the areas we have examined. It is a consistent pattern of girls' innate advantages of moral equipment and insight, of their earlier development, of their earlier and stronger autonomy, and therefore of their higher moral judgements at all ages. Only in the stark issue of life and death do boys keep anything like in step with girls in moral insight. When it comes to personal relationships – the essence of all morality – they are almost lost in the distance.

8
Religion

Morality and Religion

The relationship between morality and religion is, to say the least, confused – not least because it has never been clearly defined. Within a traditionally Christian society, the relationship of faith and morals was taken for granted. Definition, in fact, was never needed until scepticism brought with it a new basis for ethics. We see the beginnings of this modern movement away from a religious ethic in the Utilitarians of the eighteenth century. It has gone on progressively until today there is confusion in both theory and practice. New and ever increasing knowledge of the nature and workings of the universe, of nature and of man have transformed attitudes to both religion and morality.

We can best begin by defining the three general approaches to the relationship between them.

Morality Married to Religion

The traditional position holds that morality and religion are inseparable; the one flows from the other, and morality has its sole basis and justification in religion. It follows that, if religion goes, morality goes with it; nothing but moral confusion and decay can be expected when men lose their hold on religion. Hence the confusion of our time.

For such a view, moral laws are absolute, eternal and unchanging. They are given by God and laid down in the Scriptures, which, thereby, become a moral manual. They come from the transcendent, from above; all that is needed is the casuistry of applying these immutable laws to particular cases through moral theology. Hence a fixed body of 'Christian ethics', deducing man's social duties from

G

supernatural law. Such a religious code is only concerned with man
and his society indirectly. Since it has divine authority, man's duty
is heteronomous obedience to the divine moral will. The sanctions of
such a code are powerfully supernatural; and hence the strength of
religious codes, in human societies, to uphold traditional *mores* and so
to foster obedience, duty and conformity.

This traditional view, then, has three characteristics. First, it sees
morality as an outflow from religion, indissolubly bound up with it.
Secondly, without religion there can be no effective morality; for its
content, its form, its learning and its sanctions are rooted in the supernatural. Thirdly, therefore, moral decay is the logical consequence of
religious decay; if man neglects the supernatural he is morally lost.

1 The Danger of this Position

The danger of tying morality to religion has been long realised – as,
for example by Durkheim – and it is surely clear today. If religious
faith weakens, the moral code bound up with it must inevitably lose
its hold. Elements of the code may well formulate the wisdom of the
ages, derived from all man's hard won moral experience, not from
religious revelation. But, precisely because they are apparently part
and parcel of the religion, they too are thrown overboard with it.

Moreover, since such a religious code derives its authority from the
religion, and is promulgated in an authoritarian way, it loses its
sanctions when faith weakens. The question now is: 'Why?' It is no
longer enough simply to reply: 'Because God, or the Bible, or the
Church, says so.' A new approach has to be made to morality. Mean-
time, there is inevitable, if not tragic, moral confusion, when morality
is discarded with the religion to which it was bound.

2 Its Inadequacy

This transcendental morality is, moreover, clearly inadequate. It is
not only that the Bible, written over long centuries, presents many
differing moral levels – so that, for example, some children cheerfully
quote the primitive Jewish maxim, 'an eye for an eye, a tooth for a
tooth', to justify strict and rigid reciprocity. It is also clearly inadequate
as a moral handbook – which, of course, it was not intended to be. It
fails lamentably to give guidance on many crucial aspects of morality –
and not least in a scientific, urban and democratic society.

In particular, this viewpoint abuses Jesus, as Tillich puts it, in seeing him as bringing 'another, more refined and enslaving law'. The prophet proclaims timeless truths, not moral codes: principles of living, not moral rules. Hence the need of the infant Christian Church to develop an ethical code for its members, drawing substantially upon the best moral insights of its social environment; and hence the fusion of Greek and Hebraic influences in traditional Christian ethics. For example, Paul must have derived his concept of conscience from the Stoics. He also gives moral guidance to his churches. Men should obey the Roman rulers, since 'the powers that be are ordained of God'. Could this be true for Christians living under a Hitler or a Stalin? Wives should obey their husbands, Paul enjoins; but we have come to a higher view of personal relationships within marriage. Children should obey their parents, Paul teaches. But is blind heteronomy the moral ideal? Servants – that is, slaves – are to obey their masters. But Christians of later times strove for the abolition of slavery.

A static moral code would be as ineffective as a static conscience. 'New occasions teach new duties, time makes ancient good uncouth' (Lowell).

3 Conservatism

Further, this transcendental morality is inevitably conservative. By its very nature it resists change. Hence the sorry sight of organised Churches retreating reluctantly before new knowledge, instead of welcoming new truth and exploring its relevance to Christian insights. At one time, the discovery of anaesthetics was condemned as relieving man, and more particularly woman in childbirth, from the pain divinely ordained in the myth of Genesis. Today, birth-control is resisted – and that in the face of world-population explosion and of consequent large-scale famine.

For many, it is no longer adequate to quote Biblical texts or Church authorities as answering moral problems. Indeed, the very complexity of the problems raised by new knowledge and new attitudes rules out easy answers. When, for example, in terms of legal abortion, can life be held to begin? When, in terms of heart-transplant surgery, can it be held to end?

4 Moral Decay

Again, it is highly dangerous to 'prove' the indissolubility of morality and religion by holding that moral decay inevitably follows religious

decline. Such 'proof' is by no means easily found, let alone substantiated. Indeed, a completely contrary case could be made out in terms of
our own society in modern times. If there has been a decline in religious faith, our society has nevertheless become kindlier, more
tolerant, more compassionate, if still disfigured by social injustices and
moral evils. The life of the child in general, and of the illegitimate
child in particular; the treatment of the delinquent and criminal; concern for the physically and mentally handicapped; care for the socially
deprived and inadequate – all these, for example, have been transformed. If a society is to be judged by the biblical yardstick of caring
for 'the oppressed, the fatherless, and the widow', then ours is more
compassionate, despite the apparent decay in religious faith. Moreover, as William Temple stressed, social justice is the social expression
of Christian love.

The upholder of the traditional code will, no doubt, deplore
such tolerance and compassion as having opened the flood-gates to
gross abuse of the Welfare State, to widespread moral confusion, and
to rapid decline in both private and public morality. Here will be his
'proof'. For him, it seems, the ideal is heteronomy – such as is seen
in religious form in the Roman Church and in secularised form in the
Communist police state. But a democratic society must be tolerant by
its very nature; intolerant only of any ideology or conduct that
threatens to undermine it. Its broad, basic moral framework must be
defined and upheld by law; and changed only by persuasion and free
consent. Only autonomous self-rule is ultimately adequate to guide
such individual freedom.

The abuse of such freedom is 'proof', if of anything, of the breakdown of the traditional code. Once its heteronomy is challenged
or repudiated – as when the rights of individual conscience are
asserted over external authority – it is lost. Conservative, if not re-
actionary, by nature, it is unable to cope with social change, with new
knowledge that transforms patterns of living, with the new attitudes
that ensue. Contemporary moral confusion is but sorry evidence of
the growing irrelevance of a traditional, static code enforced by an
authoritarianism whose sanctions no longer hold sway.

Morality Divorced from Religion

At the opposite extreme to this transcendental view of morality, and
in reaction to it, is the view of contemporary secular humanism. It is,

broadly, an atheism that has no belief in transcendental reality. It therefore gives no place to the supernatural as the source or sanction of morality. Values are not to be tied to beliefs. They are quite distinct.

The secular humanist approach starts with man, not with the supernatural; with the needs of human society, not with any transcendental obligations. Moral duty is towards man, not towards God. Such humanism is no less concerned with morality than the religious view. But it makes morality primary, not secondary. It sees religion as impeding, not as inspiring moral progress. It sees religious intolerance as impeding, not as promoting social cohesion and well-being.

1 Religion hostile to morality

Secular humanism does not lack ammunition with which to attack religion as hostile to the moral needs of society and to moral progress.

From the past it can cite such evils as human sacrifice, sacred prostitution, taboos on valuable foods, rites of initiation that maim the adolescent, and the use of torture, killing and war to secure orthodoxy and conformity.

But it need not go back to the past. From the present it can cite the heteronomous prohibition of all forms of artificial contraception by the Roman Church as going against, not only the well-being of human society, but also the individual family in preventing planned parenthood, and in refusing sexual intercourse its sacramental nature as the expression of love. It can instance, too, religious sects that deliberately break up family life; and that refuse such medical necessities as blood-transfusion, even at the risk of death. It can quote, too, the justification of *apartheid* by a Christian Church as yet another contemporary example of inhumanity sanctioned by religion.

This is, of course, by no means the whole story. If the Christian record is marred by gross blots of inhumanity and of immorality, there is yet running through it a golden thread of humanitarianism inspired by loving care, motivated by religion. Today, for example, we take the social services for granted as natural functions of secular society. If we trace them back to their first origins, however, we find their roots watered and fed by charity – that is, love.

2 Christian and Humanist

Many, if not most, moral values are shared by both Christians and humanists, so that in many areas of social living they work together, their respective dogmatic differences being largely irrelevant. Thus, in the sphere of education, for example, it is by no means impossible for a Christian teacher to find himself supporting a humanist, and opposing a Christian, colleague in planning a school project. For they share common values; and the practical implementation of these values does not necessarily involve beliefs.

Christians and humanists would not, however, agree as to the source of these values. The fundamental question is the source of a religious, as distinct from a moral, code. Does it derive from revelation, shaping and patterning social morality? Or is it itself derived from social values and needs, giving them authority and powerful sanctions that ensure social conformity? Historically, sin, offence against God, and crime, offence against man, are by no means clearly differentiated. They have often been identified, and still are today – for example, by the majority of adults who want religious education for their children on moral grounds. But can sin and crime continue to be identified in a democratic, and therefore tolerant, society whose members may be adherents of many differing faiths, or of none, and whose various social sub-groups have varying moral codes?

The differentiation may be sought in another way. Is it possible to distinguish between characteristic religious behaviour and that of society at large? Religious outlooks vary, of course, in their prevailing tone. Some are primarily expressed in cultic activities: others in ethical demands for a specific way of life. Some are primarily concerned with individual salvation: others with the demand for social justice. One distinction made is between the ascetic and social aspects of morality. As members of a society, Christians share in its prevailing moral attitudes; and in this respect may show little difference from non-believers. There is some evidence, such as that found by Kinsey, that it is in stronger religious attitudes towards physical appetites that a difference is perceptible.

A further distinction, if less easily identifiable, is more positive. It lies in the demands made by religion for active benevolence. This is more than obedience to the practical requirements of a moral code. It is a matter of spirit, of attitude – above all, of motivation. Here is the source of the golden thread of charity that runs through Christian history, however tarnished. Here we may see the fundamental link between religion and morality.

3 The Nature of Secular Humanism

Characteristic of humanism is belief in the potentiality of human nature. Man can therefore, it holds, achieve the good life unaided: and human progress may thus be unlimited. Its stress, therefore, is upon the liberty of the individual; upon happiness as the goal of human society; upon education, above all in the sciences, as raising man above ignorance and superstition to higher planes of living. Such a Utopia will be built upon reasoning of human needs, not upon the moral demands of a revealed religion.

One of the strong appeals of secular humanism is its belief in the brotherhood of man. While religion, despite the same belief, seems to divide men into rival sects, humanism appeals to the timeless longing for universal peace and goodwill – not least in a world which science has made into one neighbourhood and, at the same time, has provided with weapons of universal destruction. Like Christianity, too, it proclaims the infinite value of each individual, regardless of his status in society or his value to it. It sees no need of religion in holding to the principle of Kant – that human personality is an end in itself, and that, therefore, no person is to be used as a means to an end.

Belief in both the brotherhood of man and the value of the individual have been traditionally derived from belief in the Fatherhood of God. Hence, for example, the inspiration of religion in striving for such reforms as the abolition of slavery. Both principles have been founded foursquare upon belief in a transcendental God to whom every individual is of value, and in whose sight, therefore, all men are equal. Can secular humanism, rejecting such a faith, find as powerful a substitute? Does it of itself possess the dynamic to actively promote and motivate these two fundamental convictions? Are they, in fact, to be attributed to human reason, to man's corporate moral experience, or to religious faith? Is secular humanism, in short, indebted to the religion it rejects for the values it proclaims?

At the very lowest, life is the supreme value to every normal human being; and taking human life, therefore, as we have found, the supreme evil in any human society. For democratic society in particular the sacredness of the individual is the supreme value; and hence derive the rights, the freedoms, and the respect due to him. Again, as we have seen from the outset, not only morality but also personality itself are only brought into being through relationships with other persons. Now the worth of the individual is an assumed value; and values have no meaning except in terms of persons. Can such values be agreed as attaching to human personality in its own right, without recourse to religion? Just as personality develops through concepts of other persons, does not the value attaching to it become recognised and valued in both self and others? In short, does not the concept of being a person include within it the recognition of the other person as an object of respect? Such an argument justifies respect for human personality solely on grounds of human rationality. To know oneself as a person is to know others as persons. It is to recognise and to respect in them the rights cherished in oneself.

Such an argument may be rationally strong. The trouble is, however, that human experience so sadly belies it. Pure reason is by no means the dominant motivating factor in human behaviour. There are powerful, irrational forces within the individual that prevent him doing even the good that he would do, and that motivate him to do even the evil that he would shun. In particular, he is not stirred by reason to respect every other person he encounters.

Such an argument, too, is supported by the instinctive sympathy that we have found even in young children, and which is the basis of all social living. Such compassion is amply and amazingly revealed in times of human disaster and suffering. But such tragedies bring out looters and profiteers, too. The milk of human kindness may flow strongly in time of distress, and in particular between those bound together by ties of race, kinship, friendship and love. But does it flow beyond these boundaries? And is it not stemmed by irrational passions and prejudices even within them? Is not antipathy as real as sympathy?

We come back, in fact, to the first basic premise of secular humanism: that man can achieve the good life unaided, and surge forward to Utopia. Reason, acting upon human experience and interpreting it in moral terms, is all that he needs. But, it seems, reason is not enough. Nor is it the sole, or even supreme, characteristic of man. If we compare him with the animal kingdom, to which he is, as we increasingly realise, intimately related, we yet find in him four characteristics that clearly differentiate him from animals. He is marked off from them by his unique sense of moral obligation; by his awareness of freedom of choice, however circumscribed; by his capacity to make personal relationships of a quality not found in the animal world; and, above all, by the capacity to stand outside himself, to transcend himself, and thus to act as his own judge, which underlies the other three. Are not these the sources of man's unique moral insights? And may they not point to a reality beyond him to which his own self-transcendence is related?

What, above all, is the source of that altruistic, self-giving love which distinguishes man at his highest? That it has its first roots in human emotions there can be no doubt. Native sympathy is the source of all human sociability. Moreover, love alone begets the capacity to love. The child who has never experienced love cannot give it; and all talk of divine love would be meaningless to him. But are such human emotions enough to inspire and motivate the highest love of goodwill, giving and seeking no return? Are they enough to inspire love of an enemy? Can they motivate going the second mile of love after the first mile of law? Can they go beyond reciprocity to selfless altruism?

Christian Humanism

The third view of the relationship between morality and religion is sometimes called the 'new morality'. It is, in fact, as old as the Gospels. Christ, it holds, did not come to replace the burden of Jewish legalism with a burden of Christian legalism. He gave principles, not rules. As the Sabbath was made for man, not man for the Sabbath, so morality was made for man, not man for morality. Persons come before moral principles; the personal morality of 'circumstances alter cases' replaces the harsh, impersonal rigidity of the legalistic morality of 'hard cases make bad laws'.

If the ethical sayings of Jesus are interpreted as a moral code, they are clearly inadequate. His is an ethic of love. Such an ethic is timeless, unconditional, and has relevance to every conceivable encounter between persons in all ages and in all societies. There must, of course, be rules for moral living. Just as autonomy grows out of heteronomy, so love builds on law. All such rules should be the expression of love; indeed, they must be judged by this yardstick. Evils are ultimately wrong, not because authoritarian rules say so, but because they deny or conflict with love. Goodness is love in action. Here is the ultimate answer to the question: 'Why?'

1 'Christian Ethics

It follows that there can be no such body of rules as to be termed 'Christian ethics'. There is but a single ethic of love, a single 'law' of love. All laws, all rules, must flow from the application of love, and be judged by it.

Two facts confirm this denial of a specific and unique body of Christian ethics. First, both as individuals and as organised Churches, Christians differ in their practical decisions upon moral issues. Indeed, there is scarcely one upon which they agree. Race-relations, marriage, birth-control, divorce, abortion, gambling, drinking – on all such vital moral issues Christians seldom, if ever, speak with one voice. There cannot, therefore, be a definitive body of Christian ethics.

Secondly, as we have seen, Christians and humanists share common moral values of the highest quality. While the Christian believes in Christ and the humanist in man, they hold common values. There is no one value that the Christian holds that a humanist could not equally hold. If there *is* a difference, it lies precisely within the realm of love. The humanist would, of course, agree in seeing love as the highest activity of human personality, and therefore as the supreme moral ideal. But Christianity is founded upon love for God, and therefore for man. Such an attitude of goodwill is unconditional in its claims. It is required for all, for both friend and foe. The explicit demand to love one's enemies is found only in the teachings of Christ. Hence the highest altruism of self-giving love, as expressed in forgiveness and in self-sacrifice.

Christianity gives, therefore, not a moral code, but moral motivation. There can obviously be moral codes without religion; every society, large or small, religious or atheist, must have some code of basic values enforced by law. But where morality is inspired by the motivation of love it is powerfully reinforced. Conversely, where the prevailing code conflicts with love, it is thereby judged and to be thereby criticised. That is the way of moral progress.

For Christian humanism, the human being is to be loved as an end in himself. It rejects the Greek, rather than Christian, dualism of body and soul. As a sacramental faith, it sees man as a body-soul, a unified personality. It is therefore concerned with the totality of man, not simply with the supposedly 'religious' aspect of his being. It is, therefore, a true humanism.

2 *Changes in 'Christian Ethics'*

The transcendental moral code is static. The ethic of love must, by its very nature, involve endless change. For it starts from the opposite end – from the nature and needs of man, and from the claims of love in meeting them.

There have, indeed, been changes throughout the centuries; and here we see religious ethics influenced by, and therefore reflecting, contemporary society. We have seen such changes in our own times – in new Christian attitudes, for example, to war, capital punishment, suicide, homosexuality, divorce. The essential values of any society abide – the prohibition of killing and stealing, for example. But Christians have certainly approved of killing, as in war and in judicial execution; and stealing, as one or two of our maturer subjects agreed with Thomas Aquinas, may be justified in certain circumstances. But it is the motivation that matters; and love is the yardstick.

This is not, of course, to say that rules are unnecessary. Heteronomy is essential; and in some measure remains so throughout life, such is the weakness of the natural self. Rules should not only teach the good; they save us from the burden of making endless moral decisions, as working rules become habits. But heteronomy is never an end in itself. Law is the schoolmaster, leading to, and preparing the way for, love. Rules are tested by love; love goes beyond them.

3 Deductive and Inductive Approaches

The transcendental moral code is deductive. It starts, that is to say, with the given, and deduces morality from it. The given is the revelation of God in the Bible; moral laws were laid down for all time on Mount Sinai and the Mount of the Beatitudes. They must be applied to all situations and persons through casuistry. They have the overwhelming authority of the supernatural. They are therefore rightly taught in an authoritarian way. Persons are, of course, subordinate to the deductive rules.

Christian humanism starts at the other end. It starts with persons, not with immutable rules. It starts where religion and morality have always started – with man, his experience, and his interpretation of it. It does not, of course, belittle revelation in its concern with personal experience; it comes closer to it. In the basic Christian experience of the Incarnation, the divine was made known in Jesus inductively rather than deductively. Acceptance of his authority, with all its claims, followed upon the experience.

Such an approach does not claim to have ready-made answers. It holds, that is to say, that the truly moral life involves responsible choice and personal decision, in the light of the overriding claims of love. Autonomy is, therefore, its moral goal.

Nor, again, does the inductive approach belittle the deductive. It seeks to become relevant by starting at the other end. It sees no easy rule-of-thumb answers to the incredibly complex moral problems of our time. It observes, too, how empirical facts – scientific, social, psychological, statistical – have changed traditional moral certainties. Above all, it takes account of the scientific and empirical world-view of our age, so radically different from that of any previous age. It therefore sees the inductive approach as the most relevant and hopeful approach for our times.

Heteronomy may well criticise such an approach as dangerous; for it lacks the consistency, the conformity, and the certainty that authority cherishes. Law is powerfully heteronomous. But even it cannot impose love – the higher morality of autonomy. Motive is the acid test of morality. It is also the dynamic of behaviour – the moral motor. To hold, therefore, that love must be the all-embracing ethic is to make perfect autonomy the moral goal.

The characteristic approach of contemporary scientific man is empirical. He asks questions, thinks in terms of cause and effect, requires proof. The inductive approach of Christian humanism is also empirical. It starts with the nature of persons and of personal relationships, and with the claims of love upon them. May not such an approach help to meet the needs of contemporary moral confusion?

Religion and Morality in the Child

This analysis of the relationship between religion and morality has been essential to our concern with development in the moral judgement of the child. We have found three alternative answers – the transcendental code, the secular humanist ethic, and the love ethic of Christian humanism. How do these relate to the child?

1 Child Studies

Studies of the place of religion in the moral development of the child have been both few and inconclusive. In general, there is slight evidence that religion does play a positive part, in both children and adults, in promoting good conduct. But the correlation is low. Moreover, from studies of offenders against the law, there is considerable overlap; by no means all delinquents have no religious affiliation.

Far stronger is the conclusion that religion is part and parcel of a way of life in the home that promotes higher morality. Thus, Hartshorne and May (1930), found that the higher conduct of church attenders was accountable, not to their attendance, but to the simple fact of their being enrolled in Sunday schools. Other studies confirm this conclusion.

It follows that other factors are involved in the familial background. Not least of these is the home discipline that we shall discuss later. We cannot, therefore, isolate religion and say that this is the positive influential factor.

There is also evidence that adolescents, like adults, conceive some relationship, however woolly, between morality and religion. 'Religion would help, if you are religious,' said one boy of 17 years; it has something, however vague, to do with 'being good'. Adolescents hold this, while rejecting the transcendental code and, indeed, much of the dogma behind it. Adults also hold this firmly, in wanting religious education for their children while themselves taking a minimal part in religious observances. Above all, there is no doubting the sincerity and earnestness of the adolescent search for values by which to live, and on which to base their relationships.

2 Isolating Religious Influence

One of the undoubtedly strong reasons for the paucity of research is the difficulty of finding objective criteria by which to assess the influence of religion upon moral judgement. Church attendance is a possible criterion, if a crude one – though it is used by the Churches themselves. We found evidence of strong positive association between church attendance and religious attitudes as derived from a 'sentence-completion' projection test. But this may mean no more than that, when churchgoing is permissive, those who attend do so because of stronger beliefs in the first place.

Another possible criterion would be the traditional Bible knowledge. But since there is strong research evidence that Bible teaching is unsuccessful even in producing Biblical knowledge, it is unlikely to have much moral influence. Children certainly cite the heteronomous Ten Commandments and the crude morality of 'eye for eye, tooth for tooth' as justifying rigid reciprocity, but seldom the Golden Rule, let alone the Gospel teaching of love. The ferment in religious education today sees clearly that many of the negative attitudes of adolescence are bred from heavy Old Testament teaching in childhood. This may well be true of morality as well as of religion.

The fact that scarcely any adolescents make reference to religion in their moral judgements may mean little. Even those specifically rejecting religion may well be indebted, though unconsciously, to religious influence in childhood. We find evidence of this influence in younger children, even if their religious expressions are verbalisms. Yet again, parents with no overt religious attitudes may well have derived their morality unconsciously, in their turn, from religious influence in childhood.

We come back again, then, to the home. The vital factors here are the values that prevail in it, both those explicitly taught, and those, even more important, that are implicitly assumed; the psychological atomosphere, expressed not least in personal relationships between parents and child; the type of discipline used, whether in the main physical or psychological; and the socio-economic background of the family, with its own characteristic moral ethos. Religion may or may not be bound up with these as one strand in the moral pattern. Even where it is, it may be repressively heteronomous rather than promoting moral maturity towards an autonomy of love.

3 Adolescent Humanism

From the onset of adolescence, the tone of children's responses is increasingly and overwhelmingly humanistic. We do find some, if minor, evidence of a rigid transcendental code, with its characteristic authoritarianism, its subordination of persons to laws, and its deductive sacred absolutes. We may instance responses to a subordinate question in the lying situation, asking whether it is worse to lie to Mother or to Father or whether it is exactly the same to lie to both. There are three categories of responses: those typically heteronomous, which naturally wane with age, but which still form 15% of responses at 17 years; those which show a warm, human relationship with one or both parents, increasing from 20% at 11 years to 62% at 17 years; and those which are coldly legalistic and which form a steady group throughout, varying between 18% and 25%.

In this instance, as elsewhere, the predominant emphasis is upon personal relationships. There are, of course, moral principles which have been learnt – undoubtedly from heteronomy – such as the prohibition of lying. But it is difficult to tell the place of religion in such heteronomy. We have indeed found evidence of religious influence in younger children. But, even at 7 years, 35% of subjects had no Church connections; and, although this figure decreases exceptionally to 25% at 13 years, it is a solid 50% thereafter. Conversely, the 60% of weekly churchgoers at 7 years decreases to 18% at 17 years.

Of responses listing outstanding virtues and vices, 5% made specific reference to 'religious good deeds', most strongly at 9 years, and with churchgoing seen as the outstanding virtue. Conversely, 'religious vices' make up 2% of responses listing bad deeds. The comparison suggests that, whilst religious practices may be admired, if more in the breach than in the observance, there is small condemnation attaching to failure to observe them. Not attending church and disobeying the Commandments head this minimal total of 'religious vices'.

If we specifically instance the ninety girls making up the 13, 15 and 17 years age-groups, only eleven find anything virtuous in religious practices, and only two find anything to condemn in their non-observance. Yet many of the virtues recognised by these subjects are profoundly religious, in the fuller ethical implications of the word. It is hard to conceive that a religious heritage had no place in shaping the recognition of such good deeds as helpfulness to the aged and the sick, and in the admiration of such qualities as giving to charity, generosity, and love of neighbour.

The tone of responses with increasing maturation is strongly humanistic. 'It all depends' is the watchword of a humanism that subordinates the rule to the person and adapts it to the personal relationship. 'It's wrong, but I would do it for love' is the ultimate definition.

The leading values of adolescents, as revealed by their ego-ideals, are self-fulfilment and contentment. The one is primarily individualistic, the other primarily social. The dreams of fame and wealth, characteristic of middle childhood, tend to wane as the realisation grows that happy personal relationships are the stuff of life. These require achieving oneself, but also denying oneself; giving, as well as getting.

A similar picture emerges from the definitions of virtues and vices. It is one of a practical, humanistic morality. The greatest virtue is to help others, the greatest vice to harm them. The virtue delineated does not go to the heights of self-sacrifice; nor vice to the depths of mental and psychological cruelty. The altruism admired is limited, tends to be local rather than universal, and is mainly within the context of actual personal relationships. If there is no great idealism, there is no inhumanity. The twin ideals are personal integrity and interpersonal amity.

The search for integrity – seen, for example, in the strenuous effort to be loyal both to the moral principle and also to the personal relationship for which it may need to be bent, if not broken – is characteristic and strong. There is a refreshing absence of formalism, of hypocrisy. The basis for this search is essentially humanistic. Heteronomy, whether with or without a religious constituent, has given the interiorised principle; humanism requires that it be adapted to the person.

If this adolescent humanism has few overt Christian roots, it is, to say the least, not opposed to the Christian humanism that subordinates rules to persons, rigidity to flexibility, and law to love. For both those with weak, and for those with strong, interiorised moral principles it is this approach – in an increasingly permissive society, and in a democratic society that does not require moral conformity – that offers the most fruitful basis for moral living. If the traditional signposts are falling down, Christian humanism may best help in finding the way. It begins with experience, with persons, with life, and with the claims of love upon them. It is positive rather than negative, inductive rather than deductive, relevant rather than remote, personal rather than legalistic, flexible rather than rigid, autonomous rather than heteronomous. Above all, it gives full place to reason in moral living; for Christian love is an attitude of the whole person – mind, heart, will. It thus takes into account every aspect of human nature. It is therefore a true humanism that may well lead on to awareness of the source of that nature – to the ground of its being.

9
Home Environment

Socio-economic Background

Psychology studies the human being primarily as an individual. Sociology studies him primarily as one of a group. We have found both insights to be essential to the study of development in moral judgement; either in isolation would be inadequate. For we have seen from the outset that the child only becomes characteristically human in human society; it alone develops his personal and moral potential into actuality. In the moral sphere, therefore, there are two essential factors – the child himself and his environment. Both heredity and environment, both nature and nurture, are intricately involved.

The development of sociology has brought out, not only the profound differences between human groupings, but also their influence upon the individual. In the moral sphere, for example, we have seen that both child and adult are, to some degree, dependent upon social praise and blame as their moral controls; and that the common definition of morality itself is conformity to the *mores* of society. But society, least of all democratic society, is not unitary in its moral outlook. There are many social sub-groupings, and therefore many codes, McDougall saw experience of differing codes as a leading factor in development towards moral maturity. In our permissive society, on the contrary, such experience may well produce moral confusion.

The term 'socio-economic' is a useful piece of shorthand to describe environment; for it indicates the breadth of the background, involving as it does both social and economic factors. A broad measure of it may be found in the five-point scale used in the national Census, based upon the father's occupation: unskilled, partly skilled, skilled, intermediate, and professional, in ascending order. The national

H

distribution curve is at its peak in the skilled class, with some 50%, tapering to the two extremes of unskilled and professional. Our sample was similar in representative make-up, though fortuitously weighted somewhat towards the lower end of the scale.

Each broad socio-economic grouping has its own characteristic outlook and consequent moral ethos and coding. Thus, a child brought up in the lowest environment may come to accept dishonesty as a natural part of his way of life, whereas a child from a higher background may well have a strong sense of honesty. The temptations, of course, are different, too. The child who is well provided for has small occasion to resort to stealing to get what he wants or needs; just as the child who is psychologically secure can afford to be much more generous in his attitude to others, as compared with the insecure and unhappy child, who may tend to be mean and fiercely punitive in judging others. There is, therefore, both economic security and psychological security. Both are reflections of the home.

Piaget and the Home

The morality of constraint, the first of Piaget's two moralities of the child, is for him the heteronomy imposed by adults that prevents moral development. Most parents, he holds, are lamentable psychologists, and the moral training that they give their children is consequently sadly inadequate. Those few parents who do seek to reason with their children, to be concerned more with motives than with consequences, can, however, achieve good and early results. Piaget recognises, too, that an affectionate mutual relationship between parent and child tends to develop a higher morality of generosity and altruism; and that guilt feelings, developing into conscience, may be aroused in a child from such a home.

But Piaget's thesis stands firm: the influence of parents is almost uniformly harmful. Their fierce and strongly irrational heteronomy, with its characteristically punitive nature, retards moral development until the child is to some extent freed from it and can develop, through free association with his peers, the second morality of co-operation. Now Piaget derived his theory from studying children from 'the poorer parts of Geneva'; and here we may see the typical *mores* of a single socio-economic class and that a lower one. Hence the inadequacy of founding a universal theory upon so narrow a basis.

Piaget, of course, was primarily concerned with the nature of the child. Nurture could hold him back, such being the typical effect of parental heteronomy. His true nature developed automatically, from within, in peer-group co-operation. Hence Piaget's rejection of many children's responses as 'adult sermons', 'meaningless formulae', 'family lectures'. He thus throws out the baby with the bath-water, refusing to see in such heteronomy the seeds of later autonomy.

Yet both of Piaget's 'moralities of the child' involved environment. He lays overwhelming stress upon nature as the supreme factor in moral development. The child's innate constitution is obviously important – as, for example, in the processes that shape the moral self and in his capacity for being conditioned. But we may well see nurture as playing the leading part in the learning of moral skills, as well as in the content of the ensuing morality.

Physical and Psychological Discipline

We may draw a broad distinction between two main types of discipline, and the results of them.

1 Physical Discipline

Physical discipline is the direct expression of adult power. It may be verbal or physical, fierce and threatening condemnation or the impulsive smack. In either case it is directed aggression. The child has learnt nothing, save that the particular offence results in punishment if detected. The discipline thus manifested is external to him. His sole concern, now, is not to repeat that offence; or, if he does, to avoid detection. He is thus dependent upon external controls. He has no further understanding of right and wrong; and thus, when temptation arises in the absence of those controls, he has no inner resources to support him in resisting it.

Such discipline is irrational. Demands are made, rules are imposed, and punishments given without explanation – even less, definition. The child is not to reason why; simply to obey. Such is the crude heteronomy that Piaget found to be characteristic of homes 'in the poorer parts of Geneva'. It certainly retards moral development, if not actually preventing it; for a child brought up under such a system of discipline may never develop an internal conscience. He remains dependent upon external rules and sanctions – upon, that is, the direction of others.

2 Psychological Discipline

Psychological discipline, by contrast, is rational. It may or may not punish, in one way or another – not necessarily physical. But it seeks to reason with the child, so that he may understand the folly of the particular offence. He is thus able to progress from the particular to the general, and to build up moral concepts – for example, consideration for others – that develop moral skills. He thus gains in moral understanding from his offences, from his moral experience; and becomes less dependent upon fear of detection and consequent punishment.

Characteristic, too, of psychological discipline is seeking to understand the child's motives for his actions, allowing for his own judgements, and encouraging him with such a measure of responsibility as he can manage. Thus, far from being at the mercy of adult whims and physical power, he learns to stand increasingly upon his own feet, in moral judgement, and so to develop towards the independence of autonomy.

Such psychological discipline is also concerned with the child's deepest needs – for love, for his ego-ideal, and for his place in his own little society. 'My Mummy says that if you tell lies no one will believe you,' says a young child; here is psychological discipline in action. The appeal may be strongly directed to one need. 'Mum and Dad told me that I ought to help people,' says a 7-year boy. Such a stress may well develop – with reciprocity adding the corollary, 'if I want them to help me' – into a conscience that is strongly concerned for others.

Psychological discipline thus tends towards an interiorised morality developing feelings of guilt that merge into conscience. The child's morality is directed from within, not from without; heteronomy progresses towards autonomy. Such a child becomes less and less dependent upon external controls, for he develops his own. He does not fear punishment from others; he punishes himself.

Mutual affection between parent and child helps this process. A child can, of course, identify with a punitive parent. Indeed, as we have seen, a fierce adult super-ego may be the vestigial voice of the aggressive, threatening, punitive parent of childhood. But identification is facilitated by a warm and mutual relationship of love; and the withdrawal of affection in disciplining may aid the internalising of parental moral values – suggest psychoanalytic studies.

3 Social Class Differences

Traditionally, physical discipline has been more characteristic of the working classes, as Piaget found, and psychological discipline more typical of the middle classes. The former leads to conformity to outward heteronomy, the latter to inculcating guilt feelings and hence to developing interior conscience. Under the one, the child becomes other-directed; under the other, inner-directed. Not only does physical discipline encourage deceit, and so defeat its own ends. The offence being expiated by punishment, no moral feelings are involved; nothing is interiorised.

It may well be that here, as in other respects, the classes are coming closer together. Moreover, strict heteronomy is against the spirit of the times, characterised as they are by questioning, if not rejection, of traditional authorities. Permissiveness, too, is no doubt involved in the weakening of heteronomy. Heteronomy is essential; and the pendulum may well have swung too far away from discipline towards a freedom that may cloak licence. But it is not least the influence of psychology that has eroded the foundations of raw heteronomy; and it is psychological discipline that alone can restore the balance.

Relationships with Parents

We found evidence for the relationships between parents and children from the Lying Test.

1 Types of Discipline

We recall, first, that whether the child would lie to his parents depended in the first place upon the relationship between them. 'If his father was vicious he would lie; if his father was understanding he'd tell the truth,' says a boy of 17 years. Another responds that he would lie because 'he'd be afraid of his father beating him'. What a contrast is the response of a girl of 15 years to the Stealing Test: 'If I did steal my conscience would prick me to tell someone, either the girl I stole from, and I would give it back, or my parents. They are very understanding, but they would be upset to think that their daughter had stolen. I've been brought up to realise that it is not right to take what doesn't belong to you.' The contrast is between physical discipline, thwarting moral development, and psychological discipline, promoting it.

2 Physical Discipline

A subordinate question, in the lying situation, asked whether it was worse to lie to Father or Mother or just the same. As noted earlier, the three types of response were heteronomous, legalistic and personal. The naturally strong 70% of heteronomous responses at 7 years have changed to the 62% of responses at 17 years that show a strong personal relationship between parent and child. But heteronomous responses remain at 15% even at 17 years.

In such responses, the authority may be either Mother or Father, or both, since 'one would tell the other, anyway'. 62% of these responses cite Father as authority, as compared with the 11%, mainly in the younger age-groups, who cite Mother. Heteronomy, then, is mainly paternal, as we would expect. Conversely, of responses based on a close personal relationship with parents, 34% cite Mother, and only 4% cite Father, the remaining 62% having a close relationship with both.

Heteronomy is naturally strongest at 7 and 9 years, and mainly physical. Father 'has a harder hand'; he would 'take off his belt'; he is 'the boss'. At 11 years he 'has more temper', 'is more stern', 'more of a boss, more frightening'. Such heteronomy wanes, but is still apparent. The contrast between physical and psychological discipline is well expressed by a boy of 13 years: 'Father would punish me more, so I'd feel more conscience about lying to my mother.' Even at 17 years heteronomy is still real for some; 'Mother would take it out on you more,' says a boy; 'Father's the one I'd get the biggest walloping from', says a girl.

3 Psychological Discipline

Such physical discipline stands as a barrier between parent and child. It prevents the 'closeness' and 'trust' of which personal responses speak. Here, Mother becomes the more important figure. While 62% speak of both parents as equally close, a further 34% cite Mother. Of the five responses showing a closer relationship with father, four are from girls, and but three of these from all adolescent subjects. Of the nineteen responses at 17 years citing Mother, fourteen are naturally from girls. But at 15 years six of the nine Mother-relationships are from boys.

This sense of personal relationship begins to develop at 11 years, with 20% of responses, increasing to 42% at 13 years and the maximum of 63% at 15 years.

Reciprocity is naturally strong at 9 and 11 years. Since Mother cares for you and does not lie to you, 'you shouldn't lie to her'; since Father pays for everything, 'you should repay him by telling the truth'. In short, 'they don't tell you lies', so that you shouldn't lie to them. But at 11 years a closer relationship is becoming manifest. 'You lose their trust. That would worry me.' Because of mutual love, 'they are both as close'. 'Father would be more hurt; Mother would take longer to forget,' says a girl. But two subjects hold that Mother would be more hurt, one on the ground that 'Father can stand up to a lie more bravely than Mother'.

At 13 years, with climacteric development, there is growing awareness of losing trust. Love is still the core of mutual closeness: 'They love you and try to help. They can't help if you lie.' There is, too, growing awareness of the hurt that may be done to parents by lying: 'They'd both be ashamed,' for 'they'd think they'd failed in bringing you up properly'. At 15 years and, again, at 17 years awareness of both breaking trust and hurting become stronger. 'It's worse to them' because 'they're the closest people to you', and 'they trust and respect you'. And strikingly different from the punitive blame of physical dicipline is the comment: 'It would hurt them both. They'd think it was *their* fault.'

Here, then, is the profound difference between physical and psychological discipline. In the former, the parents blame the child; in the latter, they blame themselves. In the one, the offending child is made to suffer; in the other, it is the parents who are hurt. It is a relationship that is broken – not a heteronomous rule. And how much stronger must be the control of the child who is conscious of the pain he would bring to loved ones by offending than that of the child who is dominated by fear of detection and consequent pain for himself.

Sex Differences

Given the innate advantages of girls in the development of moral judgement, we would expect their need of discipline to be different from that of boys. Their need is certainly different in quantity, for, as we have consistently found, boys are in much greater need of heteronomy – that is, of discipline – than girls. There is also a difference in quality, too. As psychoanalytic studies suggest, different forces are at work in girls in their interiorisation of moral values. Moreover, the traditionally different sex roles, absorbed during upbringing, must also have their bearing upon moral judgement.

We would similarly expect boys to be more dependent upon their environment than girls. We find evidence for this, particularly in regard to respect for the property of others and in the development of autonomous conscience. Moral insight may develop from intelligence, from innate sympathy for others, and from the sense of reciprocity that stems from such sympathy. Where these are not strong enough to develop moral awareness, there must be greater dependence upon external influences.

The Influence of Parents

In the home itself, parental influence is powerfully exerted upon children, and in a number of ways.

First, parents cannot help serving implicitly as models for children. Here is the source of the earliest and strongest identifications made by the child, and therefore of the values that he absorbs and makes his own. It is worth adding, too, that identification with parents persists into adult life – so that, for example, the daughter will quite unconsciously, and even contrary to her expressed intentions, reproduce in her own child-rearing practices the values absorbed from her mother. Such continuing, if unconscious, parental influence, and the conscious relationship with parents that often deepens through the years, are clean contrary to Piaget's assumption that parental controls weaken once the stage of heteronomy has been left behind.

Again, parents do give explicit moral teaching, if only in 'dos' and 'don'ts'. Such teaching may be episodic, in the context of specific situations, so that the child is given no help to form general principles. It may be impulsive, and therefore inconsistent, so that the child is given no help to form a consistent sense of right and wrong. It may, on the other hand, be reasoned, so that the child learns from each offence why it is foolish and wrong, and is thereby helped to learn inductively from a number of situations the general principle behind them. Such moral principles, whose learning takes place in a close and affectionate relationship, and whose infringement brings feelings of guilt, are the nucleus of autonomy.

There are, thirdly, unconscious moral assumptions prevailing in the home. Though seldom, if ever, spoken of explicitly, they are the more powerful for being unconsciously absorbed by the child. They stem both from the attitudes of the parents and from the moral ethos of their socio-economic grouping.

Not least important, fourthly, is the psychological atmosphere of the home. It is made up of personal relationships in the home, and therefore of the form of discipline adopted by parents in their child-rearing. In general, as we have seen, it will either develop an internal autonomy in the child, giving him his own standards of right and wrong, or it will leave him dependent upon external controls, chiefly fear of detection and of consequent punishment.

The moral learning of the child is powerfully directed by such influences in the home. For Piaget, the process is primarily a matter of maturation and of cognition, with parents only influential in so far as they impede development. We see, on the contrary, that parents are the key influences; that maturation must itself depend upon human society and the heteronomy it exerts; and that moral understanding involves not simply the mind, but also the powerful emotional factors that shape and pattern the moral self. The experiences of the child, from which he learns moral skills, are therefore of greater importance than the developmental processes at work within him.

The Influence of Socio-economic Background

The home itself is no less powerfully influenced by its socio-economic background. Each social grouping has its own moral ethos, its own values, its own code. There is evidence, for example, of higher moral judgements by children of higher socio-economic status – as in a greater concern with motivation; and of greater stress upon punishment in children of low socio-economic status. Higher status carries with it, not only its own pattern of behaviour, but a complex of advantages not enjoyed by children of low status.

Socio-economic background affects the child in shaping his development, in terms of either physical or psychological discipline, since these have had typical class associations. It also has influence in instilling the patterns of conduct that prevail in his social grouping. It decides, too, the moral values that will predominate, since those of one social class vary in their importance from those of another.

Conflict and confusion may arise, to a lesser or greater degree, as the child comes into contact with varying moral influences and values. Thus, the values of the peer group may conflict with those of the home, or the values of the home with those absorbed from mass media. Flexibility, so essential to mature moral judgement, is very different from moral confusion. The child who has learnt rational, consistent, and self-ruling principles of conduct in the home has the greater security in dealing with conflicting values, especially when they are part of the pattern of community life.

Part Three
Developmental Moral Education

10

Principles of Moral Education

Processes at Work

Morality is simply the term used to describe living together in human society. All morality, therefore, has three constituent concerns – self, others, and the relationships between self and others. As we have seen from the outset, the new-born infant can only grow into a human being in human society. Moreover, wholeness and happiness derive from relationships with others. Hence the ultimate misery of rejection and loneliness; and the ultimate punishment of a living death in solitary confinement. The castaway, the hermit, the solitary become, in some sense, less than human.

The process of moral education may, therefore, be broadly described as the socialisation of the child, shaping him into a conforming member of society. But, as we have also seen from the outset, we also use the term 'morality' to refer to the pursuit of the good life. The same term, therefore, implies both conformity to the prevailing social morality and also pursuit of an individual ideal. It follows at once that social morality must not be imposed in such a way as to prevent the possibility of forming personal ideals. We do well, again, to recall that moral progress has always been made by individuals pursuing their ideals in defiance of, and in opposition to, the prevailing moral code. It is the tight circle of imposed conformity to an authoritarian code, as in the primitive tribe, that strangles all moral progress.

If, then, morality and society are co-terminous, so that social living is saturated with moral evaluations, it is clear that no moral education is given in a vacuum. Learning morality is not like learning a foreign language, starting from scratch. It is, rather, much more like the way in which the child learns his own language, picking it up as he goes along from his environment. But the very fact of absorbing it presupposes processes at work in the child; and no attempt to analyse moral education of whatever kind can afford to ignore them. They are broad stages of child development, each with its own nature, purpose and biological value. They remain operative, moreover, throughout life, to a lesser or greater degree.

1 Imitation

We saw that the subconscious process of imitation plays an important part in the young child's development. It enables him to adapt to life by copying the actions of adults – as, for example, in the learning of language. Much is thereby absorbed that could otherwise only be learnt by laborious, and possibly dangerous, experience.

Even with development, however, there are still obvious limits to personal experience. This is true, above all, in the moral sphere, where it would be impossible to decide between different modes of action by trying out each in turn. Hence the subconscious tendency to imitate what others are doing, as in following the behaviour and fashions of the peer group.

The process of imitation works, of course, both ways. What is imitated may be good or otherwise. Influences playing upon the child – in the home, in the peer group, in the local community – are absorbed regardless of their value. The fact that 'everybody else is doing it' has its own built-in power. Not only does the child need to be one of the group and to have its esteem. He also has the instinctive feeling that its opinion is right. Hence the strength required of autonomy if it is to stand against public opinion.

The example of others is, therefore, a powerful influence, given the natural process of imitation. This applies no less to the adult than to the peer group; and no less for good than for bad.

2 Suggestion

The process of suggestion is similar to that of imitation, and follows it as an important phase in the development of the young child. It, too, is a subconscious process. But, while imitation absorbs the actions of others, suggestion absorbs emotions and attitudes. In the young child it means emotional dependence. But it, too, operates in maturity; and such dependence can be seen in the crowd, for it is the basis of the herd instinct. It is also the root of social life, both in the child's group and in the adult's circle or set, dependent upon common attitudes, fashions and opinions.

Suggestion is the more powerful for being subconscious; and it can be a powerful aid to parent and teacher. In the moral sphere it can facilitate the absorption of good personal habits and of social customs; and it is often a stronger and more effective tool than conscious instruction. Attitudes such as kindness, courtesy, and consideration can be absorbed from admired adults through this powerful process.

But it, too, works both ways. However powerful an influence in forming character, it remains essentially uncritical. As a function of the lower part of the brain, it is outside the scope of both reason and the critical faculty. While it is a natural human function, so that even strong characters may be susceptible to it, the individual who is over-suggestible will be weak in both personality and character.

Suggestion normally decreases with maturation, though stronger in the female than in the male. It is generally strong in the pre-adolescent child, and the adult can achieve much with the child by the use of suggestion – for example, in encouragement. But the very strength of the process indicates the care with which it must be used, given its irrationality. However estimable to the adult the values instilled by it may be, they may well be rejected when the critical faculty of reasoning becomes operative. Suggestion is, then, a powerful influence in the development of the moral self. But so uncertain a function may well tend towards an irrational moral code. We have held throughout that autonomy is the highest moral ideal; and such self-rule, at its best, must be both rational and critical. Moral education must seek to present moral living as reasonable living, and to promote critical assessment of different levels of conduct. Such aims demand greater care in using so irrational and uncritical a function.

3 Identification

In a further stage of development, the young child absorbs the total personality of adults closest to him; and such early identifications remain throughout life. The motives for them are love and admiration and they too remain the same throughout life. Hence, for example, the hero-worship of early adolescence in the idealisation of glamorous young adults.

Identification, again, can work both ways. Hence the importance of presenting the child with noble characters with whom he may identify. They clothe abstract ideals in concrete form; they reveal moral and spiritual truths in flesh and blood, and in human action. Hence the ageless appeal of historical ballad and chronicle, of myth and legend, of story and song, of mime and drama. The acid test of any story is the potentiality it gives for identification. All such personifications cannot help but have moral influence, through this powerful process, whether for good or ill.

4 Formation of the Ego-ideal

The process of identification is completed, finally, by absorbing the character of the loved and admired adult, so that it becomes the child's own. Hence the formation of the moral self in the child. From it flow the conflict between the moral self and the natural self, the development of self-consciousness, the self-criticism of conscience, and the growth of the self-controlling will.

Other ego-ideals are adopted during development. Adolescence, in particular, is a time of re-patterning ideals. Some may be rejected, resulting in a closer attachment to new adolescent peer values. Such new ego-ideals may well be enthusiastically adopted, either blended with the old or living uneasily beside them. The goal of all such adolescent regrouping is the striving for a recognisable, individual self. The ideal, so hard to achieve, is a complete synthesis that achieves an integrated personality, a self that is a unified whole.

We mentioned earlier the useful distinction between three 'selves' – the self as known, the self as seen by others, the ideal self. The ideal self is built up of all the identifications made throughout development, those made early with parents being generally the strongest. It is, therefore, made up of all the internalised aspirations of the individual.

Such a picture of the self, as the individual would wish himself to be, is more than aspiration. It contains a measure of obligation, of standards to be striven for in action. Such a sense of obligation is related to moral values, above all in approval or disapproval of inner desires. It may also act as a motivating factor in itself, spurring the individual to self-realisation through arduous endeavours.

The influence of adults upon this self-picture must be strong. Parents and teachers are, in the nature of things, constantly approving or disapproving, judging the child as good or bad. Hence their influence upon moral growth as the child patterns his self-portrait upon their judgements, and shapes his aspirations accordingly.

The Ideal of Personal Autonomy

It is through these basic processes that the child absorbs the values prevailing in his environment. It is through their working that the normal child develops from an amoral infant into a moral individual – moral, that is, in the broad sense of conforming to social morality. But the quality, as well as the strength, of the attitudes and values thus acquired will, of course, vary enormously. A few, never developing beyond anomy, will become anti-social deviants or psychopaths, dependent only upon the sanctions of pleasure and pain. Many will remain rooted in heteronomy, dependent upon the external controls of punishment and reward. Many more will remain fixated in tit-for-tat reciprocity, or in paying allegiance to the voice of public opinion expressed in social praise and social blame. A few will achieve the autonomy of self-direction, dependent upon neither external controls nor public opinion.

We have held throughout that personal autonomy is the highest level of moral judgement; and, in particular, that it alone is wholly adequate in a democratic and increasingly permissive society. It follows that autonomy must be the true goal of moral education.

Autonomy, however, as we have seen, may vary greatly in its constitution. We generally speak of it as 'conscience', meaning the negative super-ego rather than the positive ego-ideal. We have distinguished between types of conscience, the highest being the autonomy of inner principles that are, however, open to reason and criticism. It is an emotional autonomy that is personally independent of others; a rational autonomy that follows inner principles rather than external conventions; a behavioural autonomy that makes its own moral judgements in applying those principles to concrete situations. This must be the ultimate ideal.

The supreme characteristic of such personal autonomy is that its authority is reason. The only truly moral action, we have said, is that of a free individual, independent of all external authority, whether of private dictatorship or of public opinion. He is free, too, in having neither to conform nor to appear to conform, free from having to deceive himself or others. He has his own principles, and makes his own judgements in the light of reason. He is thereby responsible for

I

his own actions, and so develops independence and a sense of responsibility. Because such moral judgement is rational, it will bear the hallmark of consistency. Above all, it will be consistent in granting to others the rights that it possesses. Far from assuming or claiming to have the whole truth, it will be open to reasoned criticism from others.

Such are the characteristic values of personal autonomy. If we accept it as the ideal goal of moral education we can at once identify its chief enemies – processes, that is, which neither recognise such values nor seek to promote them. Three such enemies stand out from our previous discussion of the process of moral development.

1 Authoritarianism

First, of course, is the raw heteronomy that imposes the morality of obedience – the morality of the slave. It is the authoritarianism that imposes belief, or action, or both. Whether consciously or unconsciously, it denies personal autonomy. If genuine morality is the action of a free individual, such heteronomy is truly immoral.

We have seen throughout that heteronomy is essential if there is to be development towards autonomy. But this is the reasoned heteronomy that is never imposed as an end in itself. It sees itself as a means to the true end – the free, morally responsible individual. It thus seeks to make itself unnecessary. But heteronomy imposed as an end in itself is authoritarianism. It demands obedience rather than understanding; fulfilment of the law rather than concern with motives; acceptance of authority rather than self-rule. Its greatest ally is punishment. Its greatest enemy is questioning and the discussion that is simply the application of reason to moral concerns, for both presuppose autonomy. It promotes hypocrisy rather than integrity; and a rigidity in moral judgement that we have seen to subordinate persons to rules. Nor must we forget that such authoritarianism not only prevents co-operation and all the moral sentiments that flow from interpersonal relationships. It also tends to defeat its own ends; the child will lie in order to avoid the inevitable punishment.

True heteronomy is rational, in seeking to reason morality. Authority thereby attaches to the principle, not to the adult who asserts it. There is therefore, all the difference in the world between being authoritative and being authoritarian. If moral principles are reasoned, the child can accept them as being reasonable. Such reasoned authority promotes understanding and therefore autonomy. Authoritarianism, being essentially irrational, promotes neither.

2 *Physical Discipline*

Closely allied with authoritarianism, secondly, is the type of upbringing that we have described as physical discipline. It is the aggression, physical or verbal, that is the direct imposition of adult power, and that ensures and enforces obedience. It is irrational, in that the child learns nothing – save to avoid that particular offence or, alternatively, detection. It is, moreover, inevitably impulsive and inconsistent. The result is the child without moral concepts or skills who is at the mercy of adult whims and physical power. Above all, he is morally dependent upon external controls. Such an upbringing must be the enemy of personal autonomy; at the very least impeding progress towards it, if not actually making it impossible.

The contrast is with the psychological discipline that reasons morality with the child; that builds up moral concepts from particular situations; that makes motivation the heart of all morality; that encourages individual judgement and gives moral responsibility – and all this within a warm personal relationship that promotes active sympathy and all the moral emotions flowing from it. Such an upbringing promotes a personal autonomy that is not only reasoned, but also altruistic in its concern for the dignity and equality and rights of others.

3 *Indoctrination*

A third enemy of personal autonomy must be the deliberate process of indoctrination that seeks to impose upon the young child beliefs and teachings that are not founded upon, nor can ever be open to, the processes of reason. Such indoctrination is most obviously characteristic of some forms of religious upbringing. Moreover, as we have seen, the transcendental religious tradition holds that morality, too, must be similarly a matter of indoctrination. The basis of all such education is authority, whether human or – immensely more powerful – divine, and not reason. Democracy rejects such indoctrination, based upon unsubstantiated beliefs, in politics. It is coming to be seriously questioned in religion and morality, too. In particular, as we have discussed at length, the tying of social morality to religious beliefs has been a leading cause of the contemporary moral confusion.

Indoctrination denies the values that we have seen to be characteristic of personal autonomy. In terms of moral education, it could
only be harmful, dangerous and, at worst, self-defeating. As a subtle
form of authoritarianism, it not only denies the individual his rights
as a person and as a rational being. It also exposes him to the possibility of moral breakdown if and when reason asserts itself and
cracks open the flimsy foundations upon which values had been
built. Morality must be reasoned, and seen to be reasonable, if it is to
have sure foundations.

The Practice of Morality

If personal autonomy is the ideal goal of moral education, and reasoning is one of its chief characteristics, there must be a body of knowledge involved in moral education. Thus, Aristotle distinguishes
between two kinds of virtue – intellectual and moral; and adds the
practical point that, since the intellectual derives mainly from
teaching, time and experience are involved. 'Moral goodness, on the
other hand, is the child of habit, from which it got its very name,
ethics being derived from *ethos*, "habit" . . .' (*Ethics*, II.1, tr. Thomson). It is the habitual and continuous doing of right actions that
builds up the disposition to act rightly; so that the set of habits
derived from education in childhood make 'all the difference in the
world' (op. cit.).

The practice of virtuous action therefore involves three conditions:
conscious knowledge of it, deliberate willing of it 'for its own sake',
and an 'unchangeable disposition to act in the right way' (op. cit.,
II.4). Moral education must clearly be concerned with all three.

1 Knowledge

We have found ample evidence of the vital role played by heteronomy
in the development of moral judgement. Its true function, we have
concluded, is to provide knowledge of social morality, which, if
reasoned, can become progressively interiorised. The individual
acts within the limits of his moral awareness. The greater, therefore,
his moral understanding, the greater is his potentiality for moral
conduct. There is, then, an important place for moral knowledge in the
process of moral action. The child needs to learn how he ought to act.

Such moral learning assumes some level of intelligence. But we
have also seen that, while intelligence must have a key place in moral

judgement, it is by no means the only factor involved; and that, indeed, higher intelligence may in fact facilitate more clever and subtle forms of misconduct.

Again, strongly positive association between moral knowledge and moral conduct could scarcely be proved. The offences of delinquents have not generally been found to be attributable to ignorance of moral laws. Most of us, at one time or another, offend against known moral obligations, as feelings of guilt amply indicate. The motives are various: to win esteem, to avoid disapproval, to secure attention, to prove independence, to retaliate, not to mention sheer sloth and bad temper. Complete consistency in moral conduct is therefore rare, so that conduct could not be wholly and infallibly predicted. But, we have agreed, while there is specificity in moral conduct, especially in immature children and unintegrated adults, there is also that generality which alone makes it possible to speak of anyone as having a definable 'character'.

We have, further, distinguished between the cognitive and emotional aspects of moral judgement, a distinction broadly paralleling that of Aristotle between intellectual and moral virtue. Since moral concepts are strongly toned by emotion, the distinction is academic rather than realistic. Moral knowledge relates to the cognitive; and hence the fact that knowledge of the good cannot be guaranteed to be translated automatically into conduct. Such implementation of moral knowledge depends upon the orectic, non-cognitive aspects of the personality. The issue is decided by the will, the functioning of the organised self, made up of set dispositions.

2 Habit

Moral education, therefore, must be as much concerned with building up dispositions as with transmitting moral knowledge. Aristotle sees the moral virtues as being attitudes built up by repeated moral actions. They are, therefore, the fruit of habit. 'So men become builders by building, harp-players by playing the harp. By a similar process we become just by performing just actions, temperate by performing temperate actions, brave by performing brave actions' (op. cit., II.1). Moral skills, like any others, are learnt by their habitual practice.

The child is told that a certain action should, or should not, be done; and far more effectively if the wisdom or folly of the action concerned is reasoned. Thereafter, on the occasion of any similar incident, only a reminder is normally necessary to recall the moral issue involved. So good habits are built up.

The value of such habits is threefold. First, they do away with the necessity for making endless moral judgements. By becoming habitual, second nature, and more or less automatic, they by-pass many areas that would involve constant decision-making. Secondly, they build up recognisable attitudes. Many habits concern relationships with others, and so play a real part in moral conduct. Habits of kindness and courtesy, for example, shape and express attitudes towards others. Thirdly, by coping with less important and more peripheral concerns, habits leave the individual free to concentrate upon more crucial moral areas, where judgements must be conscious, deliberate and concerned.

3 Disposition

Good habits, therefore, are not the heart of morality, useful and important as they are. Good habits are valuable precisely because they have become second nature. But they are therefore limited precisely because they are not motivated by 'deliberate willing' of action 'for its own sake', nor by 'unchangeable disposition'. Virtues, says Aristotle, are not inborn capacities for feeling, nor are they the feelings themselves. They are 'states of mind in virtue of which we are well or ill disposed in respect of the feelings concerned' (op. cit.,II.5). Morality cannot be founded upon transient and, possibly, ambivalent feelings. Its only solid foundation must be deep, unchanging personal attitudes.

Here, then, is the third vital concern of moral education. Moral knowledge is vital; but it may not be acted upon. The practice of good habits helps to develop moral skills; but intimate relationships between persons involve more than moral craft. If we may again cite the adolescent's conflict between the fixed principle of truth-telling and felt obligations of friendship and love, neither knowledge nor habit nor skill are wholly adequate in reaching a decision. It is the very fact of caring for others that creates the conflict. True morality, we have said, subordinates rules to persons. It involves, that is to say, all the orectic, non-cognitive sentiments that flow between persons. Hence the vital place in moral education of the shaping of attitudes towards others.

Developmental Moral Education

Since our whole concern has been with the development of moral judgement in the child, it will be obvious that moral education must be closely geared to it. It would be as foolish to advance too far beyond the child's developmental stage as to lag too far behind it. But there are three factors that may usefully be stressed in thinking, finally, of developmental factors in the principles that must lie behind moral education.

1 Concepts

Moral thinking, like religious thinking, is simply the application of normal thought processes to a particular area of life. It must, therefore, be closely linked to the child's stage of mental development – and limited, therefore, to it. Hence, too, the place of non-moral knowledge that we have instanced by the law of cause and effect, and the crucial awareness of motivation. Conceptual development must therefore be a constant concern of moral education.

We may illustrate, negatively, from the traditional dogma of original sin. If this is interpreted as a purely religious belief, it has no relevance to moral conduct as such. But in so far as it has been taken to be manifested in moral conduct, it has ignored the normal development of the child, and not least of mental concepts. We have commented upon the enormities of cruelty to children that have flowed from this rigid dogma. Its ignorance of child egocentricity resulted in punishment of the child for 'selfishness', before he had developed concepts of others, of their separate concerns, interests and roles. Its ignorance of the child's inability to distinguish between wish and reality, flowing from the same egocentricity, resulted in punishment for 'lying' when the child was romancing. Our analysis of lying has shown how much development is required before the child can come to conceive of lying as deliberate deceit. The same dogma, too, held it necessary to break the 'self-will' of the child – that is, to break down, rather than to build up, the essential concept of self.

A positive, and crucial, example, secondly, is the concept of a person. We have said that all morality consists of relationships between persons; that its three concerns are, therefore, self, others and the relationships between them; and that the heart of morality is therefore respect for persons. The child from an early age grows in awareness of the separate identity of others, and so develops the concept of a person. But while this concept does not have to be learnt as such, it does have to be built up by moral education in terms of knowledge, habits and attitudes. To illustrate again from the lying situation, much development is necessary before the child can come to see lies as piercing the very heart of personal relationships. The ultimate aim must be to build up respect for the self-respect of others. Such a development has its basic foundation in the concept of what it is to be a person, and therefore of how to treat other persons. But if, as we have suggested, the true function of religion in the moral sphere is to motivate rather than to dictate conduct, the concept of the value of personality may be transmuted into a concept of the sacredness of personality.

2 Emotions

The key place of orectic, non-cognitive factors in moral judgement has been stressed throughout. Not least among them are the instinctive emotions. When uncontrolled and disordered, they can overwhelm reason, distort motivation, twist memory, and, of course, promote rash and impulsive conduct. But all thinking is emotionally toned. Concepts are derived from perception. Sensations arise spontaneously, but emotions are associated with perception of objects and situations. Hence the natural human process of evaluating such experience, and the emotional toning of mental concepts.

Moral education is, then, no less concerned with emotions. Negatively, there is the need for control of emotions that harm accepted social morality. This may be achieved by their suppression, especially in early stages of development; by fuller awareness of obligations to other persons; by development of the ego-ideal, and the force of self-respect; by the formation of good habits; and by their sublimation.

Positively, moral education must have as its ideal the development of worthy emotions towards both self and others. Here, too, its concern is with developmental factors, given the link between concepts and emotions. Only as concepts grow can appropriate emotions be experienced.

3 Developmental Goals

All such moral education must have developmental goals. It must, that is to say, be essentially forward-looking. Its aim being personal autonomy, it must always have that end in view in its concern with the development of moral concepts, emotions and skills.

When the child is held in the controls of heteronomy, for example, it is no function of moral education to cement him more firmly in its grip. Certainly it can seek to show the need for rules through the process of reasoning; showing, for example, how every human society has its wisdom – rulers, that is, for measuring and guiding the conduct of people towards each other. But the whole purpose of imposing discipline from without is the development of self-discipline within. Hence, for example, the constant need to give the child such responsibility as he can cope with; for only so can a sense of responsibility and self-discipline develop.

Again, when a sense of justice begins to develop with the raw reciprocity of tit-for-tat, the child's development would be impeded and hindered by concentration upon the Iron Rule of 'eye for eye, tooth for tooth'. Learning would be far more valuably centred upon higher levels of reciprocity – and not least the universal Golden Rule – as the child now develops awareness of mutual relationships with his peers.

All moral education must thus be closely geared to the overall development of the child. We can usefully think in terms of 'readiness' for moral education, in order to emphasise the vital necessity for it to be determined, at each stage, by the child's capacities and needs. Too much and too soon would be as ineffective, if not harmful, as too little and too late. Respect for self and respect for others can only be learned within the limits of the child's developmental capacities. But, given the goal of personal autonomy, both the content and the methodology of moral learning can be patterned in its light.

I I
Direct Moral Education

Indirect Moral Learning

Given that social living is saturated with moral evaluations, and that therefore no moral learning takes place in a vacuum, it is impossible to draw any limits to it. If a broad distinction may be drawn between direct and indirect moral education, it is the latter that is by far the more powerful and the more predominant. As we have seen, the moral potential of the child becomes actuality through subconscious processes; and in all the key areas of his experience indirect influences are at work.

1 The Home

By far the greatest influence upon the child's moral development is the home. It is not simply that the child spends far more of his life at home than at school or with friends. Here are made the earliest and most long-lasting identifications. Here, too, as we have amply witnessed, the child receives the greatest and most influential part of the heteronomy that will shape his moral development. Such direct moral education will be both systematic and episodic. Some, that is, will form a continuous and deliberate process of upbringing; some, too, will be on-the-spot injunctions, chiefly 'dos' and 'don'ts'. We have seen, too, the broad but vital difference between physical and psychological discipline imposed by parents, resulting respectively in an external or internal moral code.

But far more powerful than direct and explicit moral guidance are the unspoken assumptions in the home. For here concepts are formed – and not least the concept of persons. The psychological atmosphere of the home, compounded of personal relationships within it, shapes attitudes towards others. The prevailing moral values, reflecting the socio-economic background of the home, will be absorbed. It is the family that shapes personality, influences emotional development, and patterns moral concepts. It socialises the child, transmitting adult roles – behaviour patterns that the child first re-enacts in play and then ultimately reproduces in himself. In particular, sex roles are learnt – a big boy does not cry, a growing girl does not fight, for example. All this moral learning is within the context of the family pattern. The typical nuclear family of the middle classes may develop a more reasoned morality; but it may also bring its own strains through the intensity of limited personal relationships, above all that between mother and child. The large family, or even extended family, more typical of the working classes may impose a more physical discipline, but provide broader experience.

2 The School

By contrast with the immense moral influence of the home, the school may seem weak. It has far less opportunity to influence the child in terms of time. The values it seeks to transmit may be contradicted by those of the home. Moreover, teachers with a broad middle-class background may be seeking to instil a moral code alien to working-class children. But the school can provide wider social experience of adult roles for children from the limited nuclear family, and opportunity for fuller development of individual personality to children from large families.

Explicit moral education may be both systematic and episodic in the school, too. In the school assembly there is frequent assertion of moral values within the context of actual situations arising from school life. In the classroom there are frequent on-the-spot injunctions to individuals. The place of such heteronomy in the school is clearly evidenced from our responses, cited earlier. Its value lies not least in the fact that it is given within concrete situations, not in abstract and remote principles. But the growing gulf that we find, in our responses, between children and teachers may well be attributed to a heteronomy that remains authoritarian rather than aimed at developing progressive autonomy. It suggests the value of a direct moral education, based broadly on discussion, that makes reason the moral arbiter rather than the teacher.

Indirectly, the individual teacher must have immense moral

influence. Like the parent, he cannot help but serve as a model and example. As the Newsom Report commented: 'Teachers can only escape from their influence over the moral and spiritual development of their pupils by closing their schools' (*Half Our Future*, 53). Where identification is made with an admired teacher, it can be a powerful influence for good. But all his pupils are influenced by his attitude to individuals; by the system of justice that he imposes in the class-room, whether reasoned, purely heteronomous, or simply impulsive; by the fairness or unfairness displayed towards members of the class; by the integrity, or indifference, of his teaching; and, above all, by the relationship between his professions and his practice. It is, moreover, well-nigh impossible for a teacher not to indirectly betray his own values, at some time or another in whatever subject he teaches. His presentation, too, cannot but reveal whether consciously or uncon-sciously, his goal is authoritarian acceptance of his teaching or personal and reasoned autonomy.

Indirectly, the school too can exert strong moral influence. Each school has its own ethos, or atmosphere. It is formed by relationships within the school community, the head teacher playing an inevitably leading part. Relationships among the staff, between staff and pupils, and among pupils themselves are all involved, for morality is com-pounded of such personal relationships. Acid tests of such a moral ethos are not hard to seek: attitudes of teachers towards pupils, regarding them as heteronomous subjects or as potentially autono-mous persons; a sense of responsibility by older pupils for younger pupils; a pride by all pupils in the school, its tradition and reputation, and a determination to uphold its good name and esteem. Any amount of moral exhortation, whether in the context of school worship or elsewhere, will be of little avail if the moral ethos of the school contradicts it.

Of similar indirect influence will be the system of school discipline. The broad distinction is between a sacred body of objective, un-changeable rules, with categorical penalties for any infringement, and a reasoned code, seen to be reasonable, that takes account of persons, motives, relationships and personalities. It is the latter that is in keeping with the goal of the personal autonomy of internal morality. The former has the by now familiar defects of encouraging an external morality of subservience, hypocrisy and deceit. Where its sanction is physical punishment, there are two further defects. Not only does such punishment teach nothing, in that there is no moral learning in terms of developing conscience. It also develops the morally crude concept of expiation. The crime having been paid for by pain, the slate is now clean. No guilt feelings are involved; nor will they be involved should the offence be repeated. Yet, as we have amply seen, it is such guilt feelings that are essential if the child is to develop self-control and an autonomous conscience.

3 The Church

While all children are influenced by a home and a school, not all are exposed to the influence of a Church. The defects of the traditional form of direct moral instruction in both churches and schools will be our next concern. Here we may simply observe that some Churches have heteronomy as their explicit goal. Others aim at autonomy, if strongly tinged with negative guilt feelings. The ideal conscience is neither a ruthless tyrant nor a spineless slacker. Like the ideal parent, it is altruistic in its respect for the autonomy of others, rational in its openness to reason and therefore criticism, but firm in its control when personal integrity or social values are at stake. When it is motivated by the basic Christian ideal of love, it is positive, warm in human sympathy, and generous in its judgements.

The indirect influence of religion, as we have seen, is almost impossible to identify. It may well abide in national culture and permeate its institutions. It may also be differentiated in its regional influence. It may be residual in parents, as in adolescents, who have no outward religious affiliations. We have identified it as a source of heteronomy, and as part of a familial pattern of living. But that is by no means to say that the traditional feeling that religion somehow promotes social and individual morality is dead. We find it in both adults and adolescents. It has its place, however defined, as one of the indirect moral influences upon the child.

Traditional Moral Education

Direct, explicit moral instruction has been part of our national tradition. A brief analysis of its leading characteristics will be of value to our concern with direct moral education – and not least in exposing defects that must be avoided.

1 Abstract

Traditionally, moral teaching has been given in the form of abstract principles. They are, inevitably, general principles, prohibiting a vice ('Thou shalt not bear false witness') or proclaiming a virtue ('Love thy neighbour'). Piaget has made clear, in clarifying the stages of conceptual development, that before adolescence and the maturing stage of 'formal operations' any such abstract principles must be meaningless to the child. Even after adolescence by no means all have a mature capacity for grasping abstract ideas. In any case, it is highly questionable whether abstract moral principles can ever be an effective approach to moral education.

The very term 'abstract' indicates that such principles have been 'abstracted' from the moral experiences of mankind. They have derived from countless moral situations, and so become the nucleus of moral wisdom. But the individual starts with his own experience, with specific and concrete moral situations. Even if he can comprehend abstract ideas, he still has to apply them to concrete situations, either by reasoning or by actual experience. Abstract nouns, in particular, are difficult to pin down to the concrete. 'Honesty' is a vague, blanket, intangible abstraction; 'an honest boy' is far more meaningful. But an honest boy will only be recognised through his actions in a range of moral situations.

2 Deductive

The traditional approach has also been deductive rather than inductive. The virtue proclaimed has been generally substantiated by supernatural authority and transcendental sanctions. Its application has had to be deduced from it. But the individual works from the other end. He learns from his own experience – and best of all, we have seen, through the psychological discipline that has reasoned morality with him. From such experience of many concrete situations he can form concepts and build up general principles. This is the process of induction. The principle may be laid down, but it will still only become part of him through his own experience.

We may illustrate the deductive approach from traditional religious education. A passage from the Bible is read and expounded. The attempt is then made, often in vain, to apply it to the child's life today. Hence the irrelevance of so much traditional Biblical teaching, ignoring the vital interests, concerns and problems of the child.

Induction starts with them, works back to the moral principles behind them, and brings in the Bible as relevant to them.

Every moral problem involves relationships between persons; and personal relationships must ultimately involve concepts of man. Thus the inductive approach, when followed through, leads back ultimately to religious concepts. But, in contrast with the deductive approach, it does so in a relevant and meaningful way.

3 Passive

In traditional moral education, too, the child has been largely passive. It has consisted of teaching by the instructor rather than of learning by the child. It has been characteristically authoritarian, for behind it lay, not so much the moral wisdom of mankind as divine authority and sanctions. It has had to be accepted and obeyed – not discussed and reasoned.

Such teaching results, all too often, in moral verbalisms, akin to religious verbalism – in the acceptance, that is to say, of definitions that are merely verbal, that have no connections with either reason or meaning. The parrot repetition of moral maxims or religious dogmas is akin to the recitation of mathematical tables. But a meaningful concept of 'twoness' or of 'threeness' comes only from repeated experience.

Such passive moral teaching consisted of at best examples from biblical and religious history – of personifications of abstract virtues in story form; and, at worst, of purely abstract maxims. Such examples might be remote to the child in time or space, or in both. But examples from life in a distant land, in a rural setting, and in ancient times may well seem utterly remote, and irrelevant to the experience of the child in an urban, technological and scientific civilisation that cannot but pattern an entirely different world-view.

Moreover, transfer of training was taken for granted in this teaching process. It was assumed that what happened on the road to Jericho would be automatically applied by the child to the local High Street. But explicit awareness of a relationship between the two must depend upon consciousness of it. Such a connection could only be built up by making parallels between the two in concrete situations related to the child's own experience.

4 Irrational

Such traditional teaching made minimal appeal to the mind. It aimed to instil an authoritarian rather than a reasoned morality. It was essentially dogmatic; and it was assumed that, if the dogma was enforced, it must inevitably bear moral fruit. The uncritical process of suggestion would, no doubt, assist the process.

We have seen, however, that while reason is by no means the whole of moral judgement, it is a vital constituent of any effective moral learning. We have seen, too, the close relationship between moral understanding and conceptual development in the child; and, no less important, the logical connection between reason and the emotions that must have so much influence upon moral behaviour. To ignore these vital factors in moral education is to reduce it at best to conditioning, and at worst to indoctrination.

5 Negative

Such an authoritarian tradition is by its very nature heteronomous, and heteronomy tends to be characteristically negative. It is predominantly concerned with negative regulations, rather than with the positive principles that should activate good moral behaviour. It prefers, as well as requires, sticks rather than carrots, for the carrot does at least give the donkey some opportunity for autonomous action. Physical discipline is, therefore, typical of such a teaching process.

In the result, the child is dominated by fixed, sweeping, negative commandments that subordinate persons to rules and leave no room for flexibility in moral judgement. At least he learns what not to do, but the path to positive goodness remains vague and nebulous. Hence the familiar citations of the Ten Commandments by our subjects – rules that, for all their heteronomous value, remain negative, external, concerned with doing rather than with being, and have no concern with the inner motivation of the heart. By contrast, none cite the principle of love upon which Jesus based His whole teaching, and which, in its all-embracing concern with motivation, goes to the heart of all genuine morality.

6 Ignoring Conflict

The gravest weakness of traditional moral teaching has been its total disregard of the crux of the matter – the conflict of values in concrete moral situations. The powerlessness of conscience, in such a situation, is amply betrayed by the cry: 'What shall I do?'

Blind adherence to any one value is totally inadequate for moral living; and hence the weakness of blanket principles. They cannot be followed unthinkingly, for in the complex situations of life they often conflict. Indeed, such blind adherence to a single value is morally, as well as rationally, inadequate, for it ignores all the other values that may be not only relevant to the situation, but actually required by the higher moral judgement of concern for others.

Hence the need for a moral education that gives experience of weighing values against each other in concrete situations; that, through reasoning, develops critical judgement, rather than blind adherence to a moral code; and that therefore develops both moral discrimination and that flexibility which is the hallmark of moral maturity. Such an education, in short, has personal autonomy as its goal.

Direct Moral Education

A great deal of moral education is given, as we have seen, quite indirectly. Yet on all sides today we find growing interest in direct moral education in schools. The term 'moral' is, of course, often grossly limited to the area of sexual relationships. Education in such personal relationships is of the utmost importance and value; and it is a tragic commentary upon our tradition that neither education nor religion has concerned itself with the most central relationships of all human living. But morality is, of course, concerned with all relationships between persons in human society and it is the wide moral confusion of our times that arouses concern.

We may usefully ask why there should be such interest in the possibility of direct moral education. Our concern is not only with the reasons that give rise to it. We need also to be sure that the motives behind it are right. For they, in turn, will influence the approach to it.

We recall, first, the danger of tying morality to religion – that if religious faith loses its hold, the morality bound up with it loses its authority. Here is a key factor in the contemporary moral confusion. The decay of transcendental beliefs has weakened the moral code associated with them. But this code derived only in part from religious revelation as such. Associated with it is a vast store of human wisdom, hard-earned by centuries of man's moral experience. This too, loses its hold.

K

Similarly, the assumption that religious education could be relied upon to produce moral values has been found erroneous, not least after some twenty years of compulsory religious education in State schools. 'Education without religion makes clever devils,' said the bluff Duke of Wellington. The traditional answer to any concern over moral decadence in the young was more religion; stiffer doses of the well-proved medicine were the sovereign remedy. The transcendental deductive approach is no longer educationally adequate. The contemporary revolution in religious education promises hope for the future with its undogmatic open-endedness, its child-centred and inductive approach and its teaching through life-themes that ends the traditional isolation of religion, that integrates it with other aspects of the curriculum, and, above all, with life. But not all would accept association of moral education with religion; and it needs to be far more broadly based.

Again, all human beings inevitably share in the world-view of their times. Poetic myth, for example, has no meaning for our contemporary world as the ancient language of religion. The scientific outlook of our times thinks in terms of cause and effect, and is only convinced by proof. It asks the reason 'Why?', and, in the moral field, 'Why shouldn't I?' It is no longer enough to quote authorities, divine or human, or to lay down deductive laws as sufficient reason for moral behaviour. The child is inevitably conditioned by this outlook. When the language, the science, and the thought-forms of the religious world bear no relation to those of his real world there is conflict – and little doubt as to how it will be resolved.

Nor is the child helped by his experience, in a society that is morally pluralistic and permissive, of varying moral codes. Far from developing expertise in moral skills and flexibility in moral judgements, they may well breed confusion. When different authorities preach or practise different, even contradictory, codes, uncertainty may well result; one must be as good as another.

But, given the social origins of morality, moral confusion must stem from adult society. The traditional assumption is that children get effective moral education in the home. But in some homes both parents go out to work, and their children are left increasingly to their own devices. In others, popular psychology has weakened parental heteronomy. Some well-meaning parents fear lest disciplining their children may result in neurosis. The word 'discipline' itself, increasingly and significantly limited in meaning to physical punishment, has become a suspect, if not a dirty, word. Controlling the television programmes that children watch becomes dictatorial 'censorship'. Some parents abdicate their responsibility so completely as to dutifully remove themselves from the home when their adolescent children are giving a party, or leave them at home when they take a holiday abroad. They must have their 'freedom' to stay out at all hours with unknown friends. Yet such parents are astonished when they find their children in the hands of the law. Moreover, any dubious, if not hypocritical, morality of adult society, so piercingly exposed by the black-and-white idealism of youth, further weakens moral authority. So licence is mistaken for freedom; the young are given responsibility beyond their developmental capacity; above all, they are denied the opposition of firm principles that they unconsciously need, that produces creative tension, and that at least shows parental care and concern.

It is against such a background of moral confusion and uncertainty that interest in direct moral education grows. What must be its purpose? The licence of anomy, even if it masquerades as 'freedom', is no answer. Nor is authoritarian heteronomy any longer viable in a democratic and permissive society, whatever its attractions for the militaristic. The ever-growing stress upon education, seen as a value in its own right, however lacking it may be in a genuine philosophy, must at least have the effect upon the young of developing questioning, discussion, criticism – all enemies of authoritarianism. Nor, again, is the socionomy that makes morality a matter of public opinion any more viable or adequate – least of all when the public speaks with so many contending voices.

Personal autonomy remains as the only worthy and viable goal of direct moral education. While it will by no means be universally attained, it must shape the approach, the content, and the methods of all such education. Its overwhelming concern will be with persons, not with rules or social conventions, and with relationships between them. It will be rooted in reason, not in authoritarianism. Its overall concern and constant point of reference will be the moral experience of the child. Its method will be moral learning, not moral teaching.

Experience

The obvious criticism of such an approach is that the actual experience of the child is far too limited in scope. We may conclude, therefore, by differentiating between modes of experience and, in particular, seeing how they may contribute to moral education.

1 Actual

The actual experience of the child forms the primary basis. Moral situations arise from his own familiar background – home, family, relatives, school, friends, pets, games, play – and involve his interests and problems. Such situations, both actual and fictional, are concrete, realistic, and of profound relevance.

Such moral situations may be used at any age. At first quite simple, setting out a single moral problem, they may be progressively developed in their concern with motives, relationships, obligations, and circumstances.

The actual experience of children increasingly extends through the mass media. Useful material for moral education can be provided by incidents from everyday life in newspapers and magazines, fictional stories and dramas on films and on television, and by commercial advertising.

2 Imagined

The actual experience of children is being constantly extended in the classroom through imagined experience. Films and film-strips, models, loans from museums, for example, are used to enlarge its range. Here, too, are useful tools for moral education. Thus, a film on spastic children was shown to a group of C-stream children of 14 years. It was followed by the question: 'Should children like these be allowed to remain alive?' The response was electric.

What is seen makes a notoriously greater impact than what is heard; 'one on the eye is worth a thousand on the ear', as the Chinese saying puts it. This is not only true of visual aids. It is one of the many values of drama, a powerful vehicle of moral education. It has been used as such from earliest times – as, for example, in the Greek tragedies and in medieval morality plays. Drama can bring into the school varied moral situations ranging far beyond its limited concerns. It can reconstruct situations from the past or from distant settings. It can re-create situations arising in out-of-school activities in the home, in the local community, and further afield. Role-playing, in particular, is a valuable way of exposing problems of personal relationships.

The characters involved in such situations may represent a simple conflict between right and wrong, between virtue and vice. They may set out different attitudes to the same situation, and so enlarge insight. They may portray the conflict of values in the one situation. Once familiar with such an approach, children can devise situations themselves.

Discussion follows the dramatic exposure of such moral situations. It is simply the application of reason to the issues raised, chiefly motives, attitudes, and values. Experience is widened through such situations, and through discussion may come fuller understanding.

Many different types of stories have been used, through the ages, to enlarge experience through imagination on both moral and religious levels. Even the fairy stories of the young child have their moral pattern and content. Folk-tales have been a universal vehicle for transmitting accepted truth. The parables of Jesus, brilliantly constructed imaginary situations, exposed the issues at stake, and left their hearers to make their own decision. The tales of the *sufis*, the mystics of Islam, could be interpreted in depth at different levels. Fables make their own popular appeal, presenting simple morals through animals; while proverbs, story sayings, summed up the accumulated moral wisdom of the race. In all such types of stories there is rich material for moral education.

3 Contrived

Further extension of experience may be deliberately contrived, to enlarge moral awareness and understanding. Two methods are available – to give children experience of moral situations outside the school and to bring them into the classroom.

Organised visits to institutions and settings outside the school enable children to enter into situations that will be totally unfamiliar. For example, if, as we have amply seen, human society is necessary to well-being and happiness, loneliness must be a cause of great suffering and unhappiness; and it is tragically real to many of the aged. Visits to old people bring awareness of unfamiliar moral problems in society, as well as opportunities of service. So, too, do visits to children's homes. Growing adolescents need to become aware of wider moral issues than their own, to have fuller understanding of them and to be actively concerned with them. Again, visits to factories are not only a matter of possible jobs. As industrial unrest so often shows, personal relationships are vitally involved in economic life.

Alternatively, moral experience can be extended by bringing into the school individuals from various walks of life, each with his or her own special experience. Each has a role in society, however humble, and each role raises issues of social morality. Insight into the values, attitudes and motivations of various jobs and professions extends moral understanding. By providing opportunity for realistic discussion, such contrived experience explores and contrasts moral values in their social setting.

Moral Situations

We are, therefore, by no means limited to the narrow range of children's actual experience in direct moral education. Through imagined and contrived experience, the scope can be indefinitely extended.

The heart of all such education is the moral situation. It brings together values that are by nature abstract and general, and actions that are by nature concrete and specific. Indeed, moral values have no ˙ meaning or relevance except in terms of real life. It is, after all, through actual conduct that moral character is developed. Heteronomy lays down general principles of conduct, to be applied deductively. It is only through experience of real and relevant situations that children can learn their application. The inductive process is of greater value, for it starts with experience, and from analysis of specific moral actions builds up general principles. Both processes are involved in the child's moral education; each can reinforce the other.

The sources of such moral situations are many and varied, ranging far beyond real life and actual experience. Folklore and legend, fable and proverb, parable and allegory, drama and role-playing, film and film-strip, newspaper and magazine, television and advertising – all may be used as vehicles for moral learning. Their purpose is to bring to life a moral situation, to provoke discussion of it in terms of motives, attitudes and values, and, ultimately, to lead to decision.

The aim of all such moral education is not simply to enlarge moral knowledge. Certainly it seeks to provide practical experience of situations through which children may learn the basic principles and values involved in living together. But it is concerned with insight and imagination as much as with understanding, with emotion as much as with reason. Such experience, moreover, involves the shaping of attitudes and the development of moral skills. It is not reason alone that motivates action. Moral concepts involve both reason and emotion; and moral attitudes are the expression of the self. The heart of morality is care and concern for others; and hence the basic themes of all moral education – self, others, and the relationships between self and others.

12

Childhood

Developmental Learning

Our outline of the development of moral judgement in the child and adolescent has been in terms of four broad stages. We have seen, however, that these stages, far from being periods of development left behind, remain as levels of judgement. Moreover, individuals develop at by no means the same rate, and their judgements, inevitably influenced by the key variable factors, also vary from one area to another.

It follows that it would be quite false to suggest precise material for direct moral education for each specific age-group. Broad stages of development must certainly be borne in mind, so that there must be a general pattern of developmental learning. What can be done is to distinguish between the three general periods of development, and to discuss the kind of material appropriate for each.

These distinctions derive from our finding that the key period of development is between the chronological ages of about 9 and 13 years. At 7 years we find heteronomy the overwhelming characteristic. But movement towards 9 years initiates the classic period of reciprocity – between 9 and 11 years. Then, between 11 and 13 years we find the development of autonomy in terms of conscience. Thus, the climacteric period is in the middle years from 9 to 13. Here, then, will be our central period. With childhood preceding it, and adolescence following it, we have three broad periods of development.

Many would doubtless hold that adolescence is the key period for moral education. This is certainly true, above all in terms of the adolescent's primary concern for personal autonomy – typically expressed in the rebellious and critical urge towards emotional autonomy, the re-synthesis of personal values in the search for a master ideal, and the demand for behavioural autonomy as the expression of both. Adolescence is, therefore, a state of flux; and we saw evidence that at about 15 years there is a wavering and uncertainty that amply reveals it. There can thus be no doubting of the value of direct moral learning during adolescence that has personal autonomy as its goal.

The fact remains, however, that the preceding middle years form the most significant stage of development. In a real sense, therefore, this is the most creative period; and much may be done during it to assist a smoother passage through adolescence. Negatively, many pitfalls can be avoided – just as in religious education a wiser approach in earlier years can avoid many of the negative attitudes of adolescence. Positively, a fuller understanding of the moral wisdom of man, hard-earned by human experience, can provide a firmer foundation for the adolescent search for purpose and meaning that personal autonomy demands.

Here, then, are our three main periods of developmental learning in moral education. While our concern is with possible vehicles of direct learning, we must bear in mind throughout the many indirect influences, previously discussed, bearing upon the child in home and school and peer group, and forming the substance of his moral education.

Childhood

Here we are concerned with early childhood, 4 to 7 years, and middle childhood, 7 to 9 years. The enormous significance of the early years, not least in terms of morality, needs no substantiation – even if we reject the Freudian belief that moral development must be broadly complete by the age of five years. In the sense of indirect moral learning, no period is of greater importance. In terms of direct moral education, and of our three broad periods, this requires the least attention.

Within the child, the subconscious processes of imitation, suggestion, identification and the development of a moral self have all been at work. Hence the growth of an internal moral agent that may guide and, to some extent, control behaviour long before the child is consciously aware of it and able to define his conduct in terms of its functioning. In terms of moral judgement, characteristic of this period is the pre-anomy that merges with heteronomy. In the former

the child learns, from experience of pain and pleasure, on a 'prudential' or 'expedient' basis. Heteronomy artificially extends these
controls into the sanctions of punishment and reward imposed by
adults. Neither, of course, is a genuine morality.

The dominant moral theme is authority – first, that of parents, then
that of teachers, with, for many, the authority of the Church. Right
and wrong are defined by adult rulings; to be good is to be
obedient. Egocentricity is at first too strong for the development of
effective social consciousness. But the child increasingly experiences
relationships with others, becomes aware of them, and begins to form
concepts of persons. Egocentricity gradually yields to co-operation,
and hence growing awareness of rules in play.

The child learns indirectly during these early years. He also
receives much direct teaching in specific situations as they arise. But
this is spontaneous, momentary, and on-the-spot; there is, of course,
no place for anything more systematic. But we may usefully observe
the moral implications of some of his favourite materials.

1 Nursery Rhymes

Even nursery rhymes often have their own simple moral content.
Thus, Polly Flinders was punished for 'spoiling her nice new clothes'
and the Knave of Hearts for 'stealing tarts'. The three little kittens
were 'naughty' to have lost their mittens, and little Bo Peep had to
search for her lost sheep. The implications are characteristically and
naturally heteronomous.

2 Fairy Stories

Much more significance may be seen in the fairy stories so beloved of
children. Their constant appeal must be due to something more than
their charm. They may well serve to introduce the child, in the
simplest possible way, to the moral conflict that is so characteristic of
human nature.

Fairy stories have a set pattern. It begins with 'once upon a time',
and ends with 'they lived happily ever after'. In between these two
undeviating formulae, the story is of the struggle between good and
evil, personified in good people and bad people. A hero and heroine
make identification possible. They are as essential as the happy ending.
But before this is reached they endure difficulties and dangers; they
must pass through trials and tribulations.

These are the work of evil people, with evil powers, who personify the bad. The personifications of both good and evil are made crystal clear by a simple device. Good people are beautiful and evil people are ugly. Thus the prince is handsome and the princess beautiful. The witches and their like are ugly. This naïve device, so inadequate to adult experience of life, serves to distinguish good from evil. It also makes the good attractive.

The moral implications are three. First, there is a clear distinction between good and evil, and there is a struggle going on between them. Secondly, while evil is repulsive and repellent, good is attractive and desirable. Thirdly, good ultimately triumphs over evil. It is stronger than the powers of evil, despite all their fearsome, frequently magical strength.

Such stories may well project the inner experience of the child. His impulses are in frequent conflict with the rules imposed upon him by parents, and the obedience to such meaningless rules required of him. Moreover, his overwhelming need for their love demands the repression of such threatening impulses. The conflict cannot be understood, but it is none the less real, if not frightening. The conflict is projected in the fairy story; and it is defined in terms of good and evil. Here, then, is a simple introduction, in projected story form, to the moral conflict that is so deep-rooted in human experience.

3 Folk-tales

The popularity of folk-tales, too, is evidenced by the constant flow of such books from the publishers. Myth, legend and folk-tale have been universally used to transmit accepted truths; and they implicitly enshrine moral values, however dimly recognised.

Few stories have been made up simply for the sake of telling tales. The vast mass have grown up to convey human wisdom; and they may be the more powerful for their truths being implicit rather than explicit. Suggestion and identification are far more potent processes than cognition in childhood. Never are children more susceptible to the roles and examples of others, both in real life and in folk-tales from the past.

Through such stories, too, children interpret their own experiences, and build up moral values. Through them

they grope for the meaning of the experiences that have already overtaken them, savour again their pleasures and reconcile themselves to their own inconsistencies and those of others. As they 'try on' first one story book character, then another, imagination and sympathy, the power to enter into another personality and situation, which is a characteristic of childhood and a fundamental condition for good social relationships is preserved and nurtured. It is also through literature that children feel forward to the experiences, the hopes and fears that await them in adult life (*Children and Their Primary Schools*, H.M.S.O., 1967 I.595).

4 Fables

The young English child has a characteristically close sense of kinship with his animal friends. Fables have a real attraction for animal-loving people; and it was, of course, among such peoples that fables first arose. The close relationship between man and beast, at first in the essential tasks of hunting and guarding, and so later as friends, led to increasing intimacy with and understanding of animals. Naturally, the more intelligent were chosen for domestication. Animals were found to be like humans, possessing individual characteristics. Stories told of real animals inevitably led to imaginary stories in which animals were likened to, and behaved like, human beings. In time, each animal became symbolic of one outstanding vice or virtue – for example, the owl was wise, the ass stupid, the fox cunning, the wolf cruel, the pig greedy, the peacock proud, and lion brave. So the fable was born as a vehicle for conveying simple moral truths.

The 'moral' of the tale was sometimes implicit in the story itself, sometimes added as a conclusion. It was never high; sometimes, indeed, as in showing how to cheat a friend or to worst an enemy, it was not moral at all. Most fables taught a common-sense morality, always attractively, and sometimes humorously. They showed the folly of greed, pride, obstinacy, deceit, and the wisdom of being kind, honest, and hard-working.

Fables, some as old as 3,000 years, come from the Egyptians, the Assyrians, and above all the Greeks. The fables of Aesop have a long history in the West, but they could not be more popular than the fables of Pilpay in the East. The continuing attraction of fables is seen in the work of Fontaine and Krylov, John Gay and Tolstoi, Lessing and Joel Harris, Kipling and A. A. Milne.

The intimacy is close between children and animals, especially young animals. The animism of the young child is linked with anthropomorphism in his conceptualising of animals. Hence the attraction of fables for children, and their delight in animal stories in which their friends are as alive as they sense them to be. Moreover, imagination is brought into play and natural sympathy is invoked.

We are concerned here with the moral aspects of the kinds of stories loved by children, not with direct moral education as such. Thus, the fact that fables do not generally convey high moral values is not of any real significance; to use them systematically to teach such values would be totally inappropriate. But a common-sense morality is at least based upon human reasoning and moral experience; and when children are learning in daily situations that it is bad to be greedy or cruel, the exemplification of such common-sense wisdom in stories about animal friends is, to say the least, not out of keeping with their practical learning of social morality. More positively, the personification of good and evil in animals, and the projection of moral conflicts into their struggles, link the fable with the fairy story in its moral relevance, and it has, therefore, similar value.

A second possible objection to the value of fables is, of course, that if the 'moral' is to be grasped there must be some antecedent concept of the vice or virtue concerned. Such criticism clearly attached to the old-fashioned use of fables in direct moral education. It was assumed that telling the fable would automatically instil its 'moral'. But, as we have said, we are not concerned with the use of fables as vehicles of direct moral learning. It would be as useless to lay stress upon a concept – for example, of greed or cruelty – without illustrations of it as it would be to provide numerous examples of it without reference to the concept. Both are involved. If, above all, children can see parallels to their own behavioural experience in the animals' behaviour in fables, then a natural and valuable association will have been made.

Continuing Interest

There is a very definite limit, as the child grows, to interest in nursery rhymes. The same is true of fairy tales. Interest in folk-tales wanes as curiosity reaches out in ever-widening circles to the real world. Fact becomes the acid test, and fictional stories tend to become despised – unless, as we shall discuss, care is taken to examine the different types of stories, the nature and purpose of each type, and the truth that each seeks to convey.

This is not always the case, however, with animal stories. Friendship with animals may remain strong. We see it, for example, in the familiar interest in horses found in girls of about 13 years. Again, too, many children in their imaginative writing continue to choose animals as their subjects. Interest in fables may, therefore, remain; and in terms of moral learning, children might be encouraged to make up imaginative fables of their own. Exploration of collections of fables, particularly in other lands, might be encouraged. For not all fables are by any means simple and childish. Fontaine developed the fable into an art form; Krylov used fables as political weapons in authoritarian Russia; George Orwell's *Animal Farm* is scarcely a child's book.

There may, therefore, be some continuing interest in animal stories beyond childhood. But with the approach of the middle years, and of conscious moral development, far more valuable vehicles become available for moral education.

13
The Middle Years

Self, Others, and Relationships

Our evidence shows the period from broadly 9 to 13 years to constitute the time of greatest development in moral judgement. This climacteric period would, therefore, be the most creative for direct moral education. During these middle school years much may be done positively to help development towards personal autonomy, and negatively to avoid those limitations and misunderstandings that tend to cement children in lower levels.

About 9 years we observe the first apparent movement. The rules laid down by heteronomy are being universalised and internalised. A sense of reciprocity appears and is strongest between 9 and 11 years. With growing social awareness appears a sense of justice that is fiercely egalitarian in its initial stages; a conscious concern with social praise and blame; and the authority of the peer group supplements adult authority, if not competing with it. The fear born of heteronomy, dominant at 7 years, merges into feelings of guilt apparent at 9 years; and at 11 years we observe the dawn of emerging conscience. Between 11 and 13 years comes climacteric development of autonomous conscience, if earlier and stronger in girls than in boys. Here, then, is the key period of development.

With inner awareness both of guilt feelings in the self and of conscious relationships with others, direct moral education becomes possible. Its three themes, the essence of all morality, are self, others, and the relationships between them. From now on children are profoundly concerned with all three. They will be involved, with varying emphasis, in all the vehicles that seem appropriate for moral learning during this period.

Our concerns, during this period, will, of course, be determined by the child's broad development. We will comment upon them in a logical sequence – but without seeking to suggest any categorical approach.

Rules and Rulers

At the beginning of this period the child is still dominated by adult heteronomy, often of a kind that impedes moral progress. If the goal of moral education is personal autonomy, it is no part of its task to add to the force of heteronomy, or to extol its supreme virtue of obedience as the definition of moral goodness. Its concern is, rather, to examine the place and function of rules in all human society; and to discuss both the need for them, and the reasonableness of them, if we are to grow into social beings.

1 The Need to Live Together

We begin with the need to live together. The castaway on a desert island is in the apparently blissful state of being able to do exactly what he likes. But this is by no means the whole story. Attested cases of feral children show that it is only by living with others that the child is able to develop his human potentialities; the feral child remains an animal. Any isolation from other people is unnatural and bad. Examples of castaways, such as Robinson Crusoe and Ben Gunn, illustrate this truth. So do the hermits and solitaries of history, with their bizarre lives; and it was the genius of Benedict, in the West, to show that, however high their motivation, men must live an ordered life in community with others to render service to God and man.

But not only is living with others an essential condition of becoming and being human. It is also an essential condition of human happiness. Loneliness, so sadly illustrated by tragedies among the aged, is sheer misery. We recognise this by 'sending people to Coventry', the severest form of punishment by reciprocity, and a practice, therefore, by no means unfamiliar to children in their relationships. In legal punishment, solitary confinement is the most cruel of all – illustrated as the living death that it is in such stories as *The Count of Monte Cristo*. Human happiness requires relationships with others.

We must, then, live together with others. We are not just individuals; we are persons-in-society. Only the person living alone can please himself – and he is not to be envied. We cannot please ourselves, living with others, for they have the same rights as we have. How, then, are we to live together?

2 The Need for Rulers

'Rules' and 'rulers' have a common origin; both serve to measure. Just as we need rulers to measure things, so we need rulers, or yardsticks, to measure living together. As men came to live together they needed rulers and rules for their behaviour. The tribe developed its customs, the town its by-laws, the country its law code, and the empire its imperial decrees. History gives interesting examples – for example, the old Babylonian code of Hammurabi, the legislation of Moses, the laws of the Roman Republic. Naturally, we find basic similarities in codes of law. The chief concerns are offences against the person, as in killing, and offences against property, as in stealing. Less basic differences between such codes have their interest, too.

3 Wisdom Schools

Not only did men need rules for their conduct. They needed to hand on these rules to their children, and to bring them up to respect and to follow their laws. How this was done can be attractively illustrated from the wisdom schools of ancient times – in Egypt, Mesopotamia, and Israel, for example. Fascinating evidence survives, both written and visual, of the scribes and of the boys they taught, who would become the future leaders of the people. The writings and teachings of the scribes survive in the wisdom books of Egypt and Mesopotamia, and in the Jewish wisdom books in the Old Testament and Apocrypha. The striking fact revealed by this literature is the common stock of wisdom in different lands. No less impressive is the relevance of so much of their wisdom today. This is just what we should expect, as men learn the best ways of living together. But it is valuable for growing children to realise that such wisdom comes from centuries of men's living together over the world. It comes, that is, from applying reason to human experience.

4 Proverbs

The themes of all such wisdom are virtues and vices in the self, and their expression in relationships with others. They were typically expressed in proverbs – 'sayings for the world'. The proverb has always been one of the most common vehicles for transmitting moral wisdom, especially among illiterate peoples. They still have great value, as pictorial expressions of man's universal wisdom. We find

them, too, in all ages and in all parts of the world; and, while the
image used in the proverb varies from one people to another, the
truth expressed is one and the same. Children find interest in com-
paring such picture-sayings; and, from the essential re-creating of
the pictures behind each one, the common truth becomes meaningful
and understanding reinforced. Then, of course, it must be explicitly
and consciously related to a variety of concrete situations that are real
and relevant to the child, if transfer of learning is to be facilitated.

5 The Place of Rules

As throughout history, so today every human grouping needs to have
rules for living together. Hence, for example, school rules and
membership rules for youth clubs and organisations. Discussion of
all such rules is valuable. The two criteria must always be the need for
them and the reasonableness of them. Reasoning of rules, we have
noted, is an essential characteristic of psychological discipline; and
its goal is personal autonomy. Children enjoy working out rules; but
they must be tested by the essential criteria. They enjoy, too,
discussing why rules are broken, what punishments should ensue, and
what their purposes should be. Here is a useful opportunity for
developing the sense of justice.

Since general principles are almost certainly being laid down by
heteronomy, as well as specific rules, both the deductive and inductive approaches are involved during this period. In either case, the
essential need is for learning through concrete moral situations
meaningful to the child. Experience gained through them can be of
real value before he comes to the conflict that we have observed in
adolescence between the universal rule and the felt obligations of
personal relationships. Such moral learning can help the child develop
beyond a harsh and rigid legalism to a human and out-going concern
and care for others. Such concern is the essence of morality, and its
hallmark is flexibility. Moral experience, through real and felt
situations, can help to develop both.

Reciprocity

The period between 9 and 11 years is characterised by a strong but
rigid sense of reciprocity that is summed up in the constant refrain:
'It's not fair.' The aim of moral education here must be to help
children to see beyond the strict code of 'tit-for-tat' – an expressive

phrase in itself. Its origins may be interestingly traced back to the medieval 'tip-for-tap'.

This aim may be achieved by exploring different levels of reciprocity as traditionally expressed in the four 'Rules' – Iron, Tinsel, Silver, Gold. Three points need to be borne in mind in considering them. First, they are not strictly 'Rules', as the term is used in heteronomy. They are, in fact, general principles of moral action – that is, measures or rulers of conduct. Secondly, therefore, none is a substitute for an actual code of conduct. Each requires a body of derivative rules of behaviour if it is to have any relevance to daily life. Thirdly, therefore, each can only be explored and understood through application to and expression in concrete and relevant moral situations.

1 The Iron Ruler

The lowest level of reciprocity is the hard metal of iron retaliation – 'eye for eye, tooth for tooth'. We find children quoting it as melancholy proof of biblical knowledge. Its appeal is, of course, to their developmental stage. But moral education, always forward-looking, must aim to help the child see beyond it.

Examples of codes based on this principle can be found from history – for example, that of Hammurabi of Babylon and the original Mosaic code. These were early times. But, even so, this strict reciprocity was an advance on cruder moral customs, for its express purpose was to limit revenge. But it remains a primitive, low level of behaviour towards others. Its meaning and its adequacy can be explored through a variety of child situations. What does it achieve? Does it make friends or enemies? Do we like having it applied to us – for example, in punishment by strict reciprocity? Concrete moral situations can seek answers to these questions.

2 The Tinsel Ruler

An apparently higher level of reciprocity is expressed in the Tinsel Ruler – 'Treat others as they deserve'. Here, of course, concern with motives is introduced, so that this is a potential advance. But who is to decide what others deserve? It is, of course, oneself. But how can we tell what they deserve? We cannot, unless we know the inner reasons for their conduct. But how can we tell their reasons – that is, their motives? Are we, in fact, good judges of others? Do we not prejudge them – have 'prejudices', that is, that blind us? Hence the wisdom of the precept, 'Judge not, that ye be not judged.'

Practical and varied examples can explore the true nature of this principle. It turns out, on closer inspection, to be little more than the Iron Ruler dressed up; no more, in fact, than tinsel – as a piece of tinsel, kept after Christmas, will visually symbolise.

It remains true, however, that concern with motives is characteristic of higher moral judgement, beyond the horizon of strict equality. It will, therefore, be a far stronger concern of later moral learning. But concern with motives is an important aspect of psychological discipline. Exploration of the reasons for our actions, and for those of others, in actual situations can at the very least help towards the realisation that motives matter.

3 The Silver Ruler

A third level of reciprocity is summed up in the Silver Ruler – 'Do not do to others what you would not like them to do to you.' This is, of course, the negative form of the Golden Ruler, and in practice they might be explored together. But this negative expression of it does have definite psychological differences; and they indicate its limitations.

This is certainly an advance on the two previous principles. But, being negative rather than positive, it makes no demands of active goodwill. It could be fulfilled by doing nothing at all.

4 The Golden Ruler

The highest level of reciprocity is enshrined in the universal Golden Rule. Its particular form – '*What* ye would that men should do to you do ye even so to them' – is limited to specific actions. It is the general form that is of universal application – '*As* ye would that men should do to you do ye even so to them.'

Examples of this principle, whether in its negative Silver or positive Golden form, can be found in all races, religions and philosophies. For to treat others as you would wish them to treat you is the common coinage of man's universal moral wisdom. Exploration of such examples from all over the world will show that this principle is universal, that it comes from the experience of mankind through the centuries, and that it is based upon reasoning of the best way of living together with others. But, again, genuine understanding of this principle of moral behaviour can only be sought through practical and concrete examples from child life.

Sooner or later the question may be raised: Why should I treat others in this way? The broad answer is based upon human reason. No religious revelation is needed to see the common-sense wisdom of this principle of conduct. It can be motivated by reason, by enlightened self-interest. But we have seen that reason is by no means the sole constituent of morality. Motivation is the heart of the matter, and human weakness often limits the practice of the Golden Rule.

Religious motivation has therefore a real place here. It is of interest to find this principle proclaimed in all religions; and to find Hillel, the great Jewish rabbi, and Jesus himself asserting alike that it lay at the heart of religion. Natural man can know the 'natural law' – of goodwill to others, of familial duty, of justice and honesty, of truthfulness and keeping promises, of kindness and active benevolence. But these virtues may be powerfully reinforced by religious conviction. It justifies higher concern for others, provides motivation for it, and strengthens human weakness. Here religion has its own unique contribution to make to moral living.

Our evidence was that most children were quite unaware of the Golden Rule. It is useless, of course, if proclaimed simply as a general, even if sanctified, principle, as it was traditionally. To see it in action is what matters; and, given gross ignorance of it, it might be usefully derived inductively from concrete situations, and only then found from history to be universal wisdom. If the deductive method were used, the process would be reversed. In either case, its association with religion can be clearly observed.

5 The Ruler of Love

But is the Golden Rule enough? Calculations of human reciprocity can go so far. But there are two areas of profound moral concern where it would appear inadequate.

The first is the whole realm of human love. In the deepest relationships of love and friendship there is no place for calculation, for rules, for reciprocity. Love goes beyond them in giving without thought of return. It is deep-rooted in human nature. It is seen in the selfless love of a mother for her child; in the care of a 'good father' for his children, a concept that is far more than merely biological; in the love of friends for each other that dissolves self-interest in mutual identity; and in human sympathy for neighbours, seen at its best in time of trouble.

But who exactly is my neighbour? The famous parable gives the answer. Does the Golden Rule apply to everyone – to enemies, to aliens, to foreigners? In theory, perhaps, the answer is 'Yes'. But in practice it tends to be limited to 'us', and to be ignored in our dealings with 'them'. In this second area, too, something more than reciprocity is involved. Only love is adequate for it. All love must have its roots in feeling for others, in human sympathy. But this kind of love is more than feeling. It is an attitude of goodwill that at its highest is concerned for, and so cares for, enemies – those, that is, for whom there are no good feelings.

This second kind of love makes the highest demands upon human nature, for it has no feelings as such to motivate and to support it. We find it defined in the benevolence taught by Mo-ti in ancient China – teaching that was rejected for the graded reciprocity of Confucianism. We find it in the universal compassion taught by the Buddha, the *metta* that seems an inner, passive state of mind rather than an active, out-going concern for others. We find it in the love ethic of Jesus, in His demand for positive and unlimited caring, so that my neighbour is everyone. Here, too, is a close link with religion. For ultimately universal love can only be motivated by a conviction that all human beings are one family. Natural reason can of itself reach out to an ideal concept of the brotherhood of man. Natural weakness requires a motive strong enough to put it into practice by overcoming all the prejudices that divide mankind into 'us' and 'them'.

6 Levels of Reciprocity

We have followed through this sequence of levels of reciprocity to its conclusion. Two points must be added.

First, it is an evaluative sequence. It indicates, that is to say, that one level is 'higher' than another; and that love is the ultimate and highest relationship between persons. This is, of course, to discard any idea that moral education should be neutral and objective, and have no concern with comparative principles of moral behaviour. Such a rejection of moral neutrality can be justified along several lines. It is an essential characteristic of man to evaluate; pure objectivity, as psychology indicates, is a figment of imagination. Again, if morality were neutral, it is difficult to see what meaning could be attached to such terms as 'crime' and 'delinquency', 'vice' and 'virtue', 'hate' and 'love'. Nor would the exploration of morality that we suggest, in terms of human wisdom, be possible if there is really no distinction between such wisdom and human folly. The use of reason, fundamental to all morality, does not require neutrality; indeed, the analysis of moral experience that it involves rules out a neutrality that refuses to recognise comparative values.

Secondly, it is not intended to imply that this sequential account should form a rigid scheme. These levels can clearly be explored either superficially or in depth; much may be more appropriate later. There is, moreover, a wealth of material involved here that might be used under other heads. It is included here to outline a sequence that is valuable to an understanding of all human relationships – that is, of morality. All that is suggested is that at this stage children may be helped to become aware of higher levels of relationship than that of strict reciprocity; and again we emphasise that such awareness can only be achieved through exploration of concrete situations that are relevant and meaningful to the child.

Awareness of Guilt

We have seen how, during these middle years, the fear born of heteronomy merges into a sense of guilt, and that this in turn becomes the familiar concept of conscience as the inner policeman – if, broadly, the negative concept of the super-ego. The sense of guilt may well, therefore, be taken into account.

This may be done through pictorial and concrete projection in terms of a universal theme of mythology – the conflict between the godlike hero and the serpent-dragon. Ample evidence of this myth comes from many parts of the world – for example, from Mesopotamia, the Near East, Egypt, Greece, Europe and Scandinavia. There are, therefore, many versions of it, and plenty of fascinating stories to illustrate it. Such stories, to be found in many parts of the world, and with striking similarities between them, show this myth to be deep-grained in man, as Jung amply evidences.

This myth would appear to have been concerned originally with the worship of the universal sun-god, and with his triumphs over the forces of Nature. It has close links, too, with creation stories – and again with striking similarities. Only in the Far East did the concept of the dragon remain a beneficent one. For the rest of the world, the dragon came to be conceived as the symbol of evil. Thus the struggle between the godlike hero and the dragon became the struggle between good and evil. As such it came into Christianity in the struggles of heroes and saints against the forces of evil.

Such myths may be appropriate to children reaching a stage of development that brings conscious awareness of guilt feelings – that is, of conflict within the self. The universality of such a theme shows this conflict to be part of the human condition, of man as a moral being. Its projection, too, may aid understanding. The aim is not, of course, to personify the force of evil as a personal 'devil'. Such a personification will be involved in stories from various religious traditions – although it may be added that no Christian creed lays down such a belief. Moreover, children do tend to derive the concept from heteronomy; and it may have its appeal to the unconscious human capacity for myth-making. Ultimately, however, they may come to understand that both good and evil come from within; that the human being is himself the source of all vice and virtue; that man is his own tempter. But if these stories are clearly defined as myths, they do nothing to harm such ultimate understanding of the reality of evil; and by projecting the inner conflict they may help the child, at this stage, to come to recognise and to accept his inner experience of guilt.

There is ample material available here – in stories, for example, of primitive sun-gods, Ra and Apophis, Horus and Set, Gilgamesh and Marduk, Hercules and Perseus, Sigurd and Beowulf, St. George and St. Romain. Visually, we find the theme illustrated in Gothic architecture; and its imaginative gargoyles give delightful pictorial representation of vices and virtues. Not the least of the merits of medieval art are the sense of humour and the realism that makes its carvings in stone and in wood such attractive material.

The struggle between good and evil is defined in terms of virtues and vices. To catalogue them in any way would be to introduce all the defects we have found in traditional moral education. The starting-point must be the child's own experience. Children have experience of selfishness, greed, and jealousy, just as they have experience of kindness, generosity, and love. They can be recognised and identified through actual incidents, or through fictional but realistic situations. The conflict between them is real; its projection and exploration can assist understanding; and here, too, the power derived from religious motivation may be seen.

Realism

It is during this period, as the child becomes increasingly interested in the real world, that useful material can be derived from the lives of men and women of past and present.

1 Biographical Material

At all ages the lives and deeds of great men and women have their constant appeal, together with the endless fascination of human interest. But the use of biographical material – episodes, that is, rather than any attempt at complete biographies – has particular advantages during this period of development. It meets the child's immense curiosity about the real world, now that he is no longer absorbed in the world of the imagination. Again, during the stage of Piaget's concrete operations, when thinking is operationally limited to the concrete, it meets the need to present abstract vices and virtues in concrete lives and in historical situations. It meets, too, the child's hunger for romance and fascination with power. It meets his capacity and need for identification, providing material from which he can assimilate worthwhile values. Finally, by clothing the abstract in the concrete, it meets his need to see virtue in action, in real life, and not as disembodied, remote, and meaningless idealism.

Lives may be taken from all ages, from all parts of the world, and from all creeds and philosophies; for moral wisdom is timeless and universal in its concern with man-in-society. But it is vital to use contemporary biography as much as possible, so that age-old wisdom can be seen at work in the living world of here and now; and not as something lost in the mists of time that has no relevance to living together in our new and exciting world.

2 'Is it True?'

As the child becomes increasingly interested and absorbed in the real world, the question asked of any story is: 'Is it true?' Many different types of story are being met – fable, myth, parable, legend, history, and fiction. The question means, 'Did it really happen?' which, being fully interpreted, means: 'What type of story is it?'

Here is an issue of crucial importance. For, if this limitation of the term 'truth' simply to historical events is allowed to stand, the clear implication is that any non-historical story is untrue – that is, that it contains no truth and is, therefore, valueless. It is, therefore, vitally important that this asssumption is explicitly repudiated. The term 'truth' must not be permitted to be limited to mere historicity. The vast mass of human stories were made up – that is, they are non-historical. But they are true, not because they happened, but because they convey accepted truth. Such stories have been the timeless vehicles of man's spiritual and moral truth. They convey wisdom; they teach truth. Thus it is essential that the child's question is not accepted as it stands. It must be rephrased. 'What you mean is: Did it really happen?'

It is vital, therefore, that any type of story that is being used is clearly and explicitly defined. The child should be helped, during this period, to come to realise that there are different kinds of story, each with its own nature, and purpose, and meaning; and that each conveys truth. Gross misunderstandings, leading to endless trouble in adolescence, may thereby be avoided. It does not matter in the least whether a certain man did go down from Jerusalem to Jericho, for example. The timeless truth conveyed in the famous parable does not depend in the least upon mere historicity. It answers for all time the question that is the heart of all morality: 'Who is my neighbour?'

Such stories, far from being less 'true' than historical events, are much more so. Once this is realised, the various vehicles used to transmit man's wisdom down through the centuries are no longer relics of ancient fiction, to be discarded. They are of endless value.

The Analogy of Driving

There is no finer analogy of morality than that of driving on the high-way. We find it far back in history. Plato, for example, uses it of man himself. *The Chariot*, a teaching story of the Dervishes, found in Sufi schools from Damascus to Delhi, develops it in depth. With us it is driving a car. The three cardinal themes of all morality – self, others, the relationships between self and others – are involved. For living with others is exactly like driving a car on the road with other drivers. Here is a theme that can be usefully explored during this period of development.

If the driver was the only one on the road, he could, of course, like the castaway on a desert island, do exactly as he pleased. But, of course, he is not. All the principles of living with others are therefore involved.

First, the driver must know the rules of the road – those rulers that we have outlined in terms of iron, tinsel, silver and gold. He must know the rights of way, for others as for himself. They must have all the rights that he claims for himself.

The driver must also know how his car works. He must know, that is how he himself works. Here simple psychology may be introduced, possibly in parabolic form. Thus, like a car, he has a body, his physical nature. He has an engine his instinctive drives; but they must be under the control of the driver, that is the will. The driver must know where he is going, if he is not to get lost in cul-de-sacs and to be an aimless menace to others; and this direction comes from within, from conscience. Finally, the car needs petrol or 'spirit'; and this may be interpreted in terms of inner courage and determination, if not in a religious sense.

Again, the driver needs to control himself at all times if he is not to be a danger to both himself and others. Health is clearly involved – wise eating and drinking, sleeping and cleanliness. Control of feelings – temper and tongue and thoughts – is essential. So, too, is control of selfishness – of pride, of sloth, of envy, of greed – if the driver is to be fit to share the road with others. He must, in short, have self-discipline. He cannot be free to drive on the road unless he can control himself. Here is the vital lesson that there can be no freedom without discipline in any part of life.

Above all, the driver must have constant care and concern for other users of the road. He must have care for other drivers, for pedestrians, for children, for animals. He must have thoughtfulness for others, be on the look-out for them at all times. He should, too, be ready to help others, especially those in need, or involved in accidents.

Finally, the driver needs constant practice. He needs experience of all kinds of situations, to be aware of possible hazards and emergencies. He needs to develop good driving habits. He needs to learn the the prudence of practical wisdom, of wise judgement. He needs to emulate and to imitate wise drivers, those who have set a good example and are worthy to be followed.

Such a theme may be worked out on two levels. First, it may be developed in terms of social morality – of the basic essentials required of any driver on the road. Until he has them, he is not qualified to

drive. If he breaks them he is banned from the road, the characteristic punishment of reciprocity – as, for misbehaviour, the child is
sent out of the room, sent to bed, sent to Coventry.

But the theme may also be developed, secondly, in terms of the
higher meaning of morality – the pursuit of the good. A wise driver
will, of course, have all the basic essentials of driving on the road with
others. But he will not be dependent upon the controls of heteronomy,
punishment and reward. Nor will he be dependent upon the controls
of socionomy, concern for social praise and social blame. His control
will be his own inner self. If he were to act foolishly on the road, he
would be wounding his own self-respect; he would punish himself.
Nor will he ever be proud of his driving, content with himself, satisfied
that he knows everything about driving. He will always be on guard,
controlling himself, caring for others. His goal is the goal of all
genuine morality – personal autonomy.

Developmental Learning

We have dealt at length with this period of development as being a
key period, and therefore potentially creative in moral learning. By
enlarging experience, developing understanding, and promoting
insights, moral education may do much to help children progress
through it towards the goal of personal autonomy.

Both the deductive and inductive approaches may well be involved, given the sway of heteronomy. The method is essentially one of
exploration – of learning, and not of didactic, even less of authoritarian, teaching. The treatment of material used will be one of reasoning,
so far as possible, the ways in which people live together. Discussion,
spontaneous rather than organised, will therefore have an increasing
part to play, with the additional value of giving children experience of
what must be the essential methodology of moral learning during
adolescence. Above all, concrete situations, true to child life, must be
used throughout – employing, incidentally, children's imagination in
devising fictional situations that illustrate and cement their learning.

Again, there is no intention here to lay down any kind of precise
scheme or pattern for moral learning. The aim has been simply to
suggest areas which might usefully be explored during this stage of
development. Children, in any case, vary so much in their moral
experience and understanding. Some material from childhood – for
example, stories of anthropomorphised animals – may still have a

useful place. Less able children may well continue to need solidly concrete material. Some areas suggested may be of more relevance, and therefore of greater value, during adolescence; or they may be taken to fuller depth with abler children. The cardinal criterion throughout must be developmental needs; and both content and method must be patterned towards the goal of personal autonomy.

We recall, thirdly, our definition of morality as inherently evaluative – for else it is a meaningless term: and that, therefore, moral education cannot be neutral in ignoring comparative values.

But that is by no means to imply that its task is to teach values. That would simply be a return to traditional and authoritarian pedagogy. Values cannot be taught as such: they can only be assimilated. The process is essentially one of exploration by the child, learning through personal experience and, above all, personal involvement. It is only, for example, by trying out the Golden Ruler, seeing and feeling it at work in actual, imagined and contrived experience, enacting it in story and drama and role-playing, that the child may come, in any real sense, to take it into himself. Otherwise it remains at best an abstract ideal, and at worst a mere verbalism.

It follows, finally, that we are by no means simply concerned with cognitive understanding of, and assent to, moral values. They would thereby become little more than school rules – outwardly assented to during school hours, shrugged off and left behind at the close of the school day. Moral education is concerned with the whole child, not just with his mind: with the orectic, as well as the cognitive. Least of all could the Ruler of Love, for example, be learnt, let alone taught, like a mathematical formula. Only by 'getting the feel' of it – in his own personal experience, and thence in widening circles of personal relationship – can it become in any sense a meaningful reality to the child, let alone the supreme inter-personal value.

Moral education involves both comprehension and apprehension; neither can be imposed. It is wholly open-ended, recognising that genuine morality requires free personal acceptance of values – if, that is, the goal is not the heteronomy of the slave, but the autonomy of the free man.

14
Adolescence

Characteristics

In terms of our overall developmental pattern, derived from research findings, we have included early adolescence, from 11 to 13 years, within the key period of the middle years. Our concern now, therefore, is with middle adolescence, from 13 to 16 years, and with late adolescence, from 16 to 18 years.

The main process of development – whatever its quality and achievement – can now be broadly assumed. But that is by no means the end of the story. The hormones poured into the bloodstream at adolescence radically and profoundly affect the whole person. Physical changes, with the development of sexual characteristics, bring their own physical awkwardness and self-consciousness. Emotional instability, if not turbulence, brings its own problems, above all in personal relationships. Marked growth in intellectual activity is characterised by the onset of Piaget's stage of 'formal operations', bringing with it the ability to think in abstract terms to a lesser or greater degree. While security remains an essential need, the demand is for freedom to explore the expanding horizons of adolescence, and to question previously accepted conventions and the whole apparatus of adult heteronomy. In short, the search is for emotional, behavioural, and value autonomy. Later adolescence brings more developed ability for abstract thinking, and the search for ideals to which to give allegiance and around which to organise and integrate the self.

Heteronomous, authoritarian or deductive teaching is now totally inappropriate. The overriding concern is with moral experience; the approach essentially inductive; and the main method must be that of exploring moral situations through reasoning – that is, through discussion. It is such situations that must now form the bulk of the material of moral learning.

Of key significance now, too, will be relationships with adults. Heavily-charged emotional relationships in the home often prevent any possibility of confidence and trust with parents; nor is it easy for parents to let go the reins of heteronomy, and to give adolescents the responsibility they need and demand. Hence the value of an un-emotional atmosphere in the school, where problems and issues can be openly explored with sympathetic and understanding teachers, responsibility given, adolescents treated as persons in their own right, and opportunity given for service that can genuinely express adolescent idealism. Such would be the natural conditions if personal autonomy is the goal.

Methodology

The method of approach thus becomes as important as the actual content of moral learning. Outwardly the individual may appear self-assured, critical, unstable, and generally rebellious against all forms of authority. Inwardly he may well be bewildered. He has probably interiorised a body of general, abstract and mainly negative principles of conduct; and they may well be coming into conflict with newly-felt obligations of loyalty and love, in specific situations in which decision has somehow to be made. Development of the critical faculty and the unconscious search for autonomy may impel a rejection of family values; while the pressures of the peer group are increasingly claimant in their demands. If moral learning influenced peer-group values, it would thereby have greater influence over the individual.

1 Discussion

Any didactic or authoritarian approach would breed at best resentment, and at worst complete rejection. The answers of didacticism are no longer accepted on trust; adolescence questions the answers. It does so, not out of cussedness, but in the search for independence and personal values, ultimately for meaning and purpose.

The exploration of any moral concern obviously involves a body of knowledge. But it is far better found by learning rather than by teaching, by induction from real or fabricated experience rather than by deduction. Traditional rules, in particular, invite the question:

'Why shouldn't I?' The only viable approach to an answer must start from the other end – from experience, not from authority. Authority attaches to the truth being sought – not to the teacher. The teacher may be authoritative in presenting wisdom; he may not be authoritarian in asserting that he alone is right, and that therefore 'you must accept this because I say so'.

The ideal method is, therefore, full and free and frank discussion – the application of reason to moral issues. The authoritarian's denigration of discussion as 'a waste of time' simply rationalises his true purpose, however unconscious, which is to impose his own values. But values cannot be imposed; they can only be accepted. Moreover, a code that cannot face up to reasoning is gravely defective, and is better exposed. Discussion also puts into practice the basic principle of respect for personality, since each has the right to contribute, and each viewpoint is to be respected.

The method of discussion should, ideally, have already become familiar during the middle years. Previously episodic and spontaneous, it can now become increasingly systematic in moral learning.

2 Relevance

Free discussion cannot go far without exposing the interests, issues, concerns and problems of adolescence; and this is, of course, one of its supreme values. Authoritarian instruction may well be – unwittingly, of course, since it cannot know – totally irrelevant. Discussion can never be so.

It is not, nonetheless, simple, spontaneous chatting about unrelated issues as they happen to arise. Discussion must be planned. In particular, it must be based upon solid knowledge, upon facts and evidence; and this will involve research beforehand by those taking part, whether for the purpose of introducing discussion or of leading a debate. A programme of mutually agreed topics, preferably in terms of a unified scheme, will be necessary, so that discussion can be prepared and informed. It also requires skilled leadership – not only in terms of knowledge, and of guiding discussion constructively, but also in terms of eliciting participation.

Such planned discussion cannot fail to be relevant, and therefore to contribute positively to moral learning. For the issues thus exposed, and the problems explored, will be those of direct concern to the participants.

3 Induction

The process will be one of induction, moving from concrete to abstract, from particular to general, from moral situations to moral principles. Such situations, whether real or fictional, planned to form a coherent unity, will be the starting-point of exploration. This may include various activities: research into the issues involved and the facts behind them; subsequent discussion; dramatic work; role-playing; written work, especially to define and to express personal attitudes; and, not least, personal involvement in practical service expressing active concern for others.

Characteristic of adolescence, we have found, are problems arising from conflict between general rules and personal obligations. Telling lies is wrong. But what if a best friend is in trouble? Here, too, exploration of specific situations that raise such conflicts is the best way of developing moral skills in dealing with them, and, above all, of reaching decisions about them.

4 Decision

Discussion that reaches no decision, however useful in itself, is unsatisfactory and inadequate. In daily behaviour, situations in which one is involved have to be faced and decisions made. They are personal decisions. Thus, while a unanimous decision from the whole group is not to be sought for or expected, it is important that each individual should make his own.

Personal decision involves free choice; it can never be imposed. It is the function of the leader to guide discussion – but not to impose his own foregone conclusion. He may well be asked for his own evaluation; and the more so if he has a good relationship with the group. In that case it is essential that he gives his own personal decision, showing the basis upon which it has been reached. From a trusted leader this will be rightly respected, and probably influential. But it has been requested, not imposed; so that there is no conflict here with the goal of personal autonomy.

Content

It would be foolish indeed to suggest any limits to the kind of material that might form the content of moral learning during the vital period of adolescence. The needs of both individuals and groups will vary,

M

not least in terms of the broad socio-economic background. But it is possible to suggest some of the key themes that might well be involved and usefully explored.

Two initial points require notice. First, during adolescence the capacity for identification is again strong, with its unconscious search for ego-ideals. Growing idealism seeks a cause that can harness new-felt altruism, and provide a focus for self-integration. Such a cause may well be found in a leader, an admired person who inspires and calls. Many such adolescent ideals tend to be found in glamorous young adults, and increasingly so among younger adolescents. But we also find growing awareness that even such idols are only human and may have feet of clay. The striking increase in adolescents who prefer to remain themselves is an encouraging sign of greater maturity. Certainly there is still great value in biographical material – in the concrete expression of worthy values and of moral wisdom in the lives of men and women, above all in the contemporary world, who may harness adolescent idealism.

Secondly, the new sexual awareness must clearly be a key concern of moral learning. The growing revolution in sexual relationships certainly indicates the new freedom to have sexual relationships without marriage, given by increasingly effective means of contraception and of curing venereal disease. But it is also indicative of the decay of a traditional sexual morality founded upon negative fear rather than upon positive understanding of human relationships. Authoritarian rules are no longer enough; again we must start the other end, with the existential human situation, if we are to attempt any meaningful answer to the question: 'Why shouldn't I?'

Knowledge of biological facts is essential – ideally imparted before adolescence brings emotional colouring to them, and to the individual child by his parents rather than in the group. But the ideal is seldom achieved. Full understanding of the physical aspects of sex must be given by a knowledgeable and emotionally mature adult. But the facts alone are not the heart of the matter, unless we are to assume, with some biologists and psychologists, that human beings are to be equated with rats. For it is less than animal, not simply animal, for human beings to mate without personal recognition; hence at least the pretence of a 'relationship'. It is simply unhuman to have sexual intercourse on a solely instinctive basis, for it is characteristically human to use sexual intercourse, not as an end in itself, but as the expression of interpersonal relationship. Sex is a biological fact, and what matters is how facts are used. It can be used for the deepest human degradation or for the highest human happiness. Because man, as a human person, is more than an animal, the isolation of the instinctive drive is less than personal, less than human.

Hence the profound concern of adolescents with the personal relationships involved. Assuming that complete knowledge is given of the facts, in whatever context, the pre-eminent concern of moral education is with such relationships. Here yet again are the three concerns of all morality – self, others, the relationships between self and others.

1 *Understanding the Self*

Adolescents are profoundly concerned with the new selves that are beginning to emerge, and which they desperately need to understand. Traditional education has been concerned with knowledge rather than with wisdom; with facts rather than with values; with things rather than with persons. Even new approaches circle round and round the individual, giving valuable help in understanding the environment, but so seldom centring upon the individual himself. Yet if education is to be, in any genuine sense, preparation for life, it is precisely with the self that it should all begin. Learning something of the psychological make-up of the human personality could, therefore, be of immense value.

Such learning would be highly motivated, given the intense interest of the adolescent in himself. Its moral implications are wide. For example, to know something of the ways in which human beings come to think and to feel is to gain insight into the motivation of behaviour, the key to morality, and so to enlarge moral understanding. A viable, and indeed valuable, approach to such a study of the human person might be through those essential characteristics which distinguish him and mark him off from the rest of the animal creation. He is a physical being, sharing essential drives with the animal creation; and these must be the starting-point. But we go on from there, because man does. He rises above the physical world; he asks questions about it and about his place in it. He transcends, that is, both the world and himself. He stands outside himself and judges himself. It is this moral self-consciousness that is uniquely human.

So, too, is his sense of moral obligation; no other animal says to himself, 'I ought.' We feel responsible for ourselves, for others, for our behaviour to them. Hence the constant necessity for moral judgements, decisions, and consequent actions.

But they presuppose, thirdly, a sense of free will. We hear much of human beings conditioned and determined. We are, of course, conditioned by environment; and we are predetermined in some measure. Neither truth is to be sneered at. Yet this is not the whole truth. Theories of determinism, for all their attraction, do not, for example, explain why men are prepared to suffer and even to die for the sense of freedom that they cherish. Logically, too, all determinism is self-contradictory and denies itself; for, on his own theory, the determinist is himself determined. Again, all morality presupposes free will; without it there could be no sense of good or evil, of virtue or of vice. Whatever its theoretical limitations, we live by it in practice. Hence, derivatively, the vital concern of morality with the relationship between freedom and discipline.

Characteristic of human beings, fourthly, are personal relationships of a kind and quality that are unique in the animal world. They are expressed in such evaluative terms as brotherhood, community, friendship, fellowship, love; and these go to the heart of the nature of man.

Any such treatment of the psychological nature of persons must, of course, be in terms of daily living, of concrete situations, of specific human actions and motivations – above all, of the adolescent himself. Its value is not limited to moral learning. It helps towards the ideal of knowing oneself, accepting oneself, being oneself. Moreover, the growing distinction, in concepts of human nature, is not the traditional dogmatic one between theist, agnostic and atheist. It is between those who do, and those who do not, hold that man is more than a physical animal. Here, of course, is the value of such learning to religious understanding – infinitely more valuable than, say, a study of the exodus from Egypt or the journeys of St. Paul. The broad failure to develop a psychology of religion suggests an unconscious fear of modern psychology, and of what might be exposed. But if all truth is held to be of God, then there is nothing to fear. The refusal even to entertain new knowledge can only increase the isolation and assumed irrelevance of religion; and so leave the field to half-truths and to limited insights.

Hence the wide value of a study of the human person, in the light of modern knowledge and in terms of his unique characteristics. They point beyond him, beyond the strictly moral. Indeed, every moral concern involves a basic concept of the human person, of his nature, purpose, and destiny; and it is with the search for meaning and purpose that the adolescent is increasingly concerned.

2 *The Nature of Love*

We have seen that the highest measure of relationships between persons is the yardstick of love. No word in the English language has been more abused, if only because of the vast burden of interpretation laid upon it. Here is a key concern of the adolescent, as well as of morality. Definition of the nature of love is valuable, and it may best be attempted in terms of Greek concepts of it.

Eros is natural, instinctive love. It may be defined as passion. Its whole concern is with getting what it desires. Typically, such desire is sexual; but a passion for, say, money can be no less 'erotic'. Morally, this is the lowest kind of love, since it seeks to get rather than to give.

But, since human beings are persons, rather than simply animals, this instinctive drive is spiritualised, romanticised, idealised. In sexual relationships it forms the basis of a personal love that is commitment to sharing life together. *Philia* defines such relationship of mutuality between persons. It is morally higher because it not only seeks to get, it also gives.

The highest kind of love is that which gives, seeking no return. The obscure Greek term *agape* had to be taken over to define the love-ethic of Jesus, and so to be given a rich content. Such love is pure self-giving; an attitude of goodwill, the expression of the whole self. That it is not simply emotional is clearly indicated by the injunction to love enemies – those who by definition are not liked emotionally. It is essentially an attitude of will, the functioning of the organised self.

A far more comprehensive definition and application of these Greek concepts is given by C. S. Lewis (*The Four Loves*, Bles, 1960). Their moral development is the progressive elimination of self. But the psychology of their development is no less important. Since the highest love must have its roots in the lowest – for it presupposes the human capacity to love – no level is to be despised. If, as McDougall suggests, mother-love is the root of all altruism, instinctive human love has its own deep moral colouring and potentiality. Traditional dualism, despising the body as the source of evil and exalting the soul, contrasted the baseness of physical passions with the purity of divine love. Such a dichotomy is false psychologically, for human nature works as a unity. It is false morally, since the capacity for and comprehension of love must be rooted in human nature. The fundamental point is the nature of the person and of personal relationships.

3 *The Nature of Personal Relationships*

Levels of such relationships between persons can be usefully defined in the personalism of Martin Buber. Simply expressed, we can distinguish between three types of relationship.

First is the I–IT relationship. Here the 'I', the self, treats the other person as an 'IT' – that is, as a thing. There is no relationship as such; for the other person is not treated as a person, but used as a thing. He or she is depersonalised, used by complete egotism for self-satisfaction. An example is the treatment of human workers as mere 'hands', an expressive term, in the heyday of the Industrial Revolution; another is the use of a woman in prostitution. Here is, in fact, human slavery – using persons as depersonalised things.

Far more truly human, secondly, is the I–YOU relationship. Here is a genuine relationship between the 'I', the self, and the plural 'YOU', the group of others. The relationship is a co-operative one with others, as in most social groupings – the home, the school, the club, the society, the community. Here there is genuine mutuality, for all members of the group are treated as persons. There are mutual rights and obligations, there is giving and taking, in living or working together as a group. Such terms as 'brotherhood', 'fellowship', and 'community' are evaluative definitions of such a group personal relationship.

Highest of all is the I–THOU relationship between two individuals. Each treats the other as a person in his or her own right, and in the fullest sense. Here is complete respect for the value, if not the sacredness, of human personality. Here is complete mutuality, complete self-giving, holding nothing back. Here, as we noted, is one of the unique characteristics of man as man. Here is the source of the highest human fulfilment and happiness – the source of friendship and of love.

These different types of relationship must, again, be not merely illustrated, but defined in terms of real life. They can serve as a useful yardstick of the relationships that adolescents make in all areas, not only in the sexual. But their relevance to relationships between the sexes is profound. Sex and religion are the two universal experiences by which human beings can transcend themselves, reach beyond themselves, have the vision of eternity; hence the romantic's conviction that his love will be 'for ever'. The decay of religious faith has led to the search for self-fulfilment and self-transcendence being made, all too often, through sex alone. It then carries a burden which it is not capable of bearing; and the result, too often, is inevitable disillusionment. Sex is a means to an end, not an end in itself. It is rightly used as a vehicle of expression of love between persons. But such love is a relationship in which persons are treated fully as persons – never as things.

4 Moral Situations

Personal relationships will thus play a large part in the content of moral learning in adolescence. They must, as we have insisted throughout, be approached through concrete examples – through moral situations, whether taken from real life or fictional. Their nucleus will be actual experience, extended through imagined and contrived experience. But there are many varied sources available for such situations – for example, films, television, radio, novels, plays, advertisements. Exploration and discussion of such situations could do much to develop moral skills, understanding, and insight, and thereby to influence moral attitudes.

But morality is not only concerned with the purely personal; it has far wider, social concerns. There is a danger in so emphasising the personal – as, for example, in stories such as parables which treat solely of the individual – as to lose sight of wider moral applications and therefore obligations. The healthy, increasing concern of many adolescents with wider problems of society and of the world has an integral place in moral education. They are no longer content with parochialism, in religion or politics or any other area of life. Much adolescent idealism is no longer focused upon the parish pump. It breeds vehement criticism of traditional institutions and attitudes. It is also one of the most hopeful signs of the times. A world that modern communications have made into one neighbourhood desperately needs to be made into one brotherhood. Moral learning must have this wider concern.

Late Adolescence

In the final stage of adolescence, from 16 to 18 years, the operational capacity for abstract thought is fully developed; and hence the search for ideals, although concrete moral situations still have a valuable part to play. Frustrated idealism becomes cynicism. It is bred by any authoritarianism which denies responsibility, self-discipline and free discussion – which refuses, that is, freedom to develop personal autonomy.

Given inevitable differences of understanding, as well as of moral experience, some of the essential topics already mentioned may well have a place at this stage.

1 Abstract Concepts

There may not now, however, be so great a need to approach every issue through concrete examples. Discussion may now be in terms of abstractions – of such often burning issues as justice and freedom. But they are, of course, abstracted from human experience, and have no meaning without concrete human relevance. Hence discussion of current issues, in the light of such abstractions.

Such discussion can have great value in moulding moral ideals and attitudes. But it can remain theoretical if it has no relation to active concern and care for others.

2 Search for Meaning and Purpose

The strong need for integration in self-fulfilment requires goals; and hence the search for meaning and purpose in life. Maturing capacity for abstract thought and strong idealism both relate to this search. The nature, purpose and destiny of man may become leading concerns in this search for a philosophy by which to live.

Religion is strongly involved. Characteristic of our times is the failure of traditional answers, and of their expression in traditional organisations and modes of worship, to have meaning and relevance for the young. Yet on all sides there is evidence of acute interest in religion. In such a confused and pluralistic society, the approach must be open-ended. It can make no given assumptions, lay down no unchallengeable laws – if, that is, religious autonomy is the goal. The approach must be existential and inductive; for much traditional theology is necessarily characterised by concepts, thought-forms and language that are meaningless to contemporary man, with his world-view so radically different from that of any previous age. Interest grows in world religions, as well as in non-religious ideologies, such as secular humanism and Marxism. There can be no imposed limits to discussion if the search for meaning and purpose is to be genuinely honest and autonomous.

The relationship between religion and morality, previously analysed, may have a key place in this search. We have suggested that the true function of religion is in motivating, rather than in dictating, morality. We have also suggested that every moral issue is ultimately a religious issue, since it involves persons and therefore a concept of the nature of persons. But the concept may be non-religious, as in contemporary secular humanism; and, moreover, morality as such does not need religion for its existence. There is, therefore, a wide area for discussion; and here, too, it must be open-ended.

3 *Study of Moral Development*

Relevant to such discussion would be an understanding of the process of moral development. Such a study covers a wide area, involving as it does psychology, sociology, ethics and religion. It thus has additional value in being the meeting-ground of a number of disciplines each of which must be myopic on its own.

It can, secondly, usefully help the individual to become aware of the influences that went to shape his existing moral attitudes. If elements of irrationality survive, they can at least be seen to be irrational. But irrational prejudices and immature attitudes may also be exposed; and conscious awareness of them may thus help progress towards moral maturity.

Again, such a study is the most hopeful one in the search for meaning and purpose, if the only viable approach today is through induction, through the life of man-in-society. It is intensely practical, relevant, and absorbing in its concern with self and others. It also gives opportunity for reaching back to ultimate values that must determine concepts of the nature, purpose and destiny of man.

Finally, such a study brings fuller awareness of the levels upon which human beings conduct their lives; and therefore the possibility of greater understanding and insight. It can thereby aid the development of that moral maturity which is the hallmark of responsible citizenship in democratic society.

Select Bibliography

Moral development

EPPEL, E. M., and M., *Adolescents and Morality*, Routledge & Kegan Paul, 1966.

HARTSHORNE, H., and MAY, M. A., *Studies in the Nature of Character*, I-III, New York: Macmillan, 1928-30.

HAVIGHURST, R. J., and TABA, H., *Adolescent Character and Personality*, New York: John Wiley, 1949.

KOHLBERG, L., *The Development of Children's Orientations Towards a Moral Order*: I, *Sequence in the Development of Moral Thought*; II, *Social Experience, Social Conduct, and the Development of Moral Thought*. Basel: Vita Humana, 1963, 1964.

PECK, R. F., and HAVIGHURST, R. J., *The Psychology of Character Development*, New York: John Wiley, 1960.

PIAGET, J., *The Moral Judgement of the Child*, tr. Gabain, Routledge & Kegan Paul, 1932.

STEPHENSON, G. M., *The Development of Conscience*, Routledge & Kegan Paul, 1966.

Moral education

CASTLE, E. B., *Moral Education in Christian Times*, Allen & Unwin, 1958.

HEMMING, J., *Moral Education in Chaos*, ed. Raison, *Youth in the New Society*, Rupert Hart-Davis, 1963.

NIBBLETT, W. R., ed., *Moral Education in a Changing Society*, Faber & Faber, 1963.

WILSON, J., *Approach to Moral Education*, Oxford: Farmington Trust, 1967.

—— *Aims of Education in Religion and the Emotions*, Oxford: Farmington Trust, 1967.

—— *et. al.*, *Introduction to Moral Education*, Penguin Books, 1967.

Ethics

ARISTOTLE, *The Nicomachean Ethics*, tr. Thomson, Penguin Books, 1955.

FIELD, G. C., *Moral Theory*, Methuen University Paperbacks, 1966.

HOSPERS, J., *Human Conduct*, New York: Harcourt, Brace & World Inc., 1961.

PETERS, R. S., *Ethics and Education*, Allen & Unwin, 1966.

Philosophy

DEARDEN, R. F., *The Philosophy of Primary Education*, Routledge & Kegan Paul, 1968.
HARE, R. M., *The Language of Morals*, Oxford University Press, 1952.
RAMSEY, I. T., ed., *Christian Ethics and Contemporary Philosophy*, S.C.M. Press, 1966.
REID, L. A., *Philosophy and Education*, Heinemann, 1962.
SINGER, M. G., 'The Golden Rule in Philosophy', *Philosophy*, XXXVIII, No. 146, 1963.

Psychology

HADFIELD, J. A., *Psychology and Morals*, Methuen University Paperbacks, 1964.
—— *Childhood and Adolescence*, Penguin Books, 1962.
McDOUGALL, W., *An Introduction to Social Psychology*, Methuen University Paperbacks, 1960.

Sociology

MACIVER, R. M., and PAGE, C. H., *Society*, Macmillan, 1964.
MUSGRAVE, P. W., *The Sociology of Education*, Methuen, 1965.

Psychoanalysis

FLUGEL, J. C., *Man, Morals and Society*, Penguin Books, 1962.

Education: General

ALVES, C., *Religion and the Secondary School*, S.C.M. Press, 1968.
ELVIN, H. L., *Education and Contemporary Society*, Watts, 1965.
Newsom Report, *Half Our Future*, Chapter 7, H.M.S.O., 1963.
Plowden Report, *Children and Their Primary Schools*, H.M.S.O., 1967.

General

JEFFREYS, M. V. C., *Personal Values in the Modern World*, Penguin Books, 1962.
LEWIS, C. S., *The Four Loves*, Bles, 1960.
MACMURRAY, J., *Reason and Emotion*, Faber & Faber, 1935.
ROBINSON, J. A. T., *Christian Morals Today*, S.C.M. Press, 1964.

Index